The Independent Woman

The Independent Woman:

How to Start and Succeed in Your Own Business

Rae Wisely and Gladys Sanders

J. P. Tarcher, Inc.
Los Angeles
Distributed by Houghton Mifflin Company
Boston

Library of Congress Cataloging in
Publication Data

Wisely, Rae.
  The independent woman.

  Bibliography: p. 161
  Includes index.
  1. New business enterprises. 2. Women in
business.
I. Sanders, Gladys.   II. Title.
HD62.5.W53   658.1'141   81-50009
ISBN 0-87477-176-5   AACR2

J. P. Tarcher, Inc.
9110 Sunset Blvd.
Los Angeles, CA 90069

Library of Congress Catalog Card No.: 81-50009

Design by Jane Moorman

MANUFACTURED IN THE UNITED STATES OF AMERICA

P 10 9 8 7 6 5 4 3 2 1

*To J. B. Nethercutt, a pioneer in
recognizing and encouraging the entrepreneurial
spirit in women*

CONTENTS

The Independent Woman

Open, Sesame!

ou could call this book a spontaneous happening. It came about as the result of a small-business seminar sponsored by Merle Norman Cosmetics, a seminar that, in its first year, attracted thousands of ambitious women in cities across the country. Women of all kinds, from all walks of life, of all ages and backgrounds; teachers, homemakers, secretaries, professionals, salespersons; women with jobs in middle management, young women just out of college, widows in their fifties, women looking for something meaningful to do, divorcées with young children, singles with none, women earning substantial salaries, women yearning to make the leap into a higher bracket.

Even with their diversified backgrounds, these women all had one thing in common: a desire to explore the golden opportunity of being their own bosses—a desire to be entrepreneurs.

In a sense these wonderful audiences were our collaborators, because in answering the sophisticated and searching questions they put to us, we learned what most concerned them. As a result, the seminars grew in depth and stature—so much so that three universities asked us to give them under their auspices.

At the end of every seminar wherever we went—San Francisco, Hartford, Boston, Cleveland—at least a dozen women would come up and ask us to make it into a book that they could take home and read at their leisure. So here it is. The book they asked for.

We offer it as a general introduction for both the novice and the aspiring entrepreneur. As such, it includes a discussion of the issues a woman must consider when starting a business, the classic problems that most new owners face, and some equally classic solutions to these dilemmas, along with some strategies of a more unusual nature. We have also included for illustration and instruction the stories of a number of women who have created thriving enterprises. But their experiences, inspirational though they may be, are not our primary interest. Our focus is instead on the actual process of launching a business and making it a success.

One of the themes that you will see repeated throughout this book is the importance of reaching out to secure good professional advice and personal support. In our own endeavor we were especially fortunate in this regard. Therefore, we would like to express our deepest appreciation to several people within the Merle Norman organization as well as to others who also served as our advisers. It was their generosity in sharing time and expertise that made this book possible.

Our thanks go first to Gary Hollister, president of Merle Norman Cosmetics. His straight-from-the-shoulder talk on entrepreneurship provided us with background for the opening chapters as well as a broader perspective on the entire subject.

Arthur Armstrong, secretary and general counsel to Merle Norman and senior member of the law firm of Armstrong, Hendler and Barnet, gave us the invaluable legal advice that we pass along to you in Chapter 3.

Mike Hayes, senior vice president of finance at Merle Norman, assisted us in the preparation of the sections on accounting, record keeping, and using your accountant as a valued adviser.

Merilyn Vande Griff-Burnside, a director of the Far West Bank in Tustin, California, a financial consultant to small businesses, and a loan officer at United California Bank, Los Angeles, gave us information and assistance in planning and writing "Money Demystified—A Capital Subject" and "La Boutique—A Sample Business Plan."

To Doris Tarrant, president of the United Jersey Bank in Montvale, New Jersey, goes the credit for the dollars-and-sense advice on how to make a friend of your banker and negotiate a bank loan.

Terri Erspamer generously shared with us her expertise on choosing locations and negotiating leases. Terri is the director of new studio development at Merle Norman.

The help in "Help Wanted" came from David O'Conner, senior vice president in charge of personnel and education at Merle Norman. His background includes conducting more than seventy-five seminars in business management.

And the input for "Letting the World Know—The Power of Advertising and Public Relations" came from seasoned pro Gordon Maynard, a vice president of public relations at Merle Norman cosmetics.

Special thanks to J. B. Nethercutt, Merle Norman's chairman of the board, for his generous support of the small-business seminars.

And a salute to our creative editor, Millie Loeb, whose perceptive blue pencil kept us on target.

The Independent Woman is about translating dreams into profit-making realities. It warns you about the pitfalls and the perils, tells you about the satisfactions and rewards of being your own boss, and outlines what it takes, where to go for help, how to assess your chances, how to measure your motivation. It can't guarantee your success, but it can point you in the right direction. All of us who collaborated on this project hope it proves an open sesame to many of you.

Rae Wisely
Gladys Sanders

CHAPTER 1

A Dozen Women Who Made It

omen are ingenious, inventive, and, says psychologist Robert May, more tuned in to new social trends than men. Set a thoughtful woman in an office where she observes the rapid turnover of secretarial help, and in due time she launches a successful secretarial school. Take two artists with an inside view of what other artists are looking for, and you get a multi-million-dollar picture-frame company. Confront a Norwegian-born schoolteacher with the energy crunch, and she harks back to the wood-burning stoves of her childhood, sets about getting the exclusive rights to import them, and is off to a six-figure-a-year business.

Give still another woman a couple of hanks of wool, some scraps of fabric, an artful eye, and agile fingers; before long she's running a lucrative cottage industry from her home. That's not to say a home-based business has to be a craft, though: a recent national survey found that women working at home are producing everything from cookies to couches, and one was customizing vans in her backyard.

Take a group of lively, gregarious women who enjoy lunching out and live in a neighborhood with no place to lunch in. Or an intelligent young woman crazy about antique wicker and tired of a nine-to-five job. Up come a restaurant and a wicker boutique. Put a young divorcée in a situation where she has to support herself and a child, and she ends up running four lucrative cosmetic studios.

The women you'll meet in the next few pages are not unique. They represent more than a million like them who are running a wide variety of successful small businesses across the country. And their number is growing by leaps and bounds as women become more confident, more assertive, more aware that a business of one's own beats working for the other guy or gal.

These are gutsy women who know how to capitalize on experience, build on a dream, scent out a new business opportunity. Ambitious, motivated, and nonstop workers, they have the courage of a contender, the bounce back of a trampoline. Success is their destination!

Pamela McGinley Scurry

Her Business Is . . . Antique Wicker

The Wicker Garden on the upper East Side in Manhattan lives up to its name. It's a veritable garden of lacy wicker—armchairs, side chairs, sofas, étagères, tea carts, prams, and tables, some of them rare turn-of-the-century pieces, all in pristine condition.

Pamela McGinley Scurry, with a graduate degree in teaching and computer technology from Boston University, left her job as an executive editor at Harcourt, Brace and Jovanovich at twenty-nine because, as she says, "I wanted the satisfaction of being my own boss; I wanted to see if I could make it on my own." She got a $10,000 personal loan from a bank and rented space that she and her husband renovated and painted.

Scurry invited every newspaper and magazine home-furnishings editor in New York, New Jersey, and Connecticut to her opening and provided them with good photos and news releases. Since then, almost every major national magazine in the field and every New York newspaper has run a feature on the Wicker Garden.

How successful she's been can best be judged by the fact that two years after she opened her shop, she was able to buy the building it's in. Nor did all her profits come from the sale of antique wicker. She "accessorized" her shop. A pram had its own flowery quilt and was filled with pillows and dolls, one more beguiling than the next; chairs and sofas were decorated with one-of-a-kind pillows; tables held hand-painted lamps with custom-made shades. When customers bought a wicker piece, they usually bought the whole caboodle, accessories and all. As a result, Scurry developed a wholesale line of gift items—pillows, quilts, lampshades, dolls—made by forty-five talented women who work in their homes and keep her supplied with unique hand-made items.

Two years ago, after her son was born and she found it difficult to find classic baby clothes at a moderate price, she decided to remedy the situation and opened the Wicker Garden Baby over her original shop. On weekends she and her husband take off to go "wickering" as far north as Maine, as far south as the Carolinas. What happens to the baby? He comes along—in a wicker basket, of course.

The Factors of Success

1. She went into business just as nostalgia for the "country look" made wicker particularly prized. Her own collection of antique wicker gave her a head start.
2. She maintains excellent relations with the press. "If a magazine calls at 4:30 in the afternoon to say they want a particular item to photograph at 9:00 A.M. the next day and they want it in a particular color scheme, we'll stay up all night to have it ready."
3. Every piece of wicker she sells has been reconditioned and put into tip-top condition so that it presents no problem to the buyer.

4. She built up a corps of forty-five to fifty free-lance craft persons who supply her store and her wholesale business with fresh, unusual, and exclusive pillows, throws, dolls, lampshades, and other decorative accessories.
5. She diversified quickly. The Wicker Garden Baby shop and the wholesale business have multiplied the profitability of her initial shop many times over.

Frieda Caplan

Her Business Is . . . Produce

If you enjoy the papayas, jicamas, and sunchokes you now find at your local supermarket, you can thank innovator Frieda Caplan, founder and president of Frieda's Finest, Specialist in Exotic Produce. In 1957 Caplan, who had been working as a cashier in the Los Angeles fruit market, found herself selling mushrooms as a sideline. Soon she came to know every mushroom grower and supplier in Southern California. In 1962, when space became available in the Los Angeles market, she was urged to go into business, and Produce Specialties was born. Its purpose: to develop and promote the unusual and different in fresh fruits and vegetables.

Mushrooms are still her number one item and the base of her business, but Caplan takes the greatest pride in the new fruits and vegetables she has introduced: papayas from Hawaii, kiwis from New Zealand, Jerusalem artichokes (which Caplan renamed sunchokes), jicamas, chayote squash, lemon cucumbers, pearl onions—a whole gamut of new taste delights now regularly appearing on America's tables as a result of one woman's imagination and drive.

How did she do it? "It's been an educational job all the way," she says. "First, we had to educate the produce men in the markets. We had to prove to them that food editors influence women's buying habits. When food editors talk about papayas or kumquats, it behooves markets to stock them, or customers will go elsewhere to find them."

She developed point-of-purchase material. She packaged new items with recipes and storage instructions. She circularizes every food editor in the United States with articles, pictures, and recipes featuring each new product she launches.

In 1979 Caplan was elected Produce Marketer of the Year, the first woman to hold that title. She's added 50,000 square feet of facilities to her enterprise. Her eldest daughter, Karen, who majored in agricultural economics at the University of California, is now in the business with her, as are twenty-four other full-time employees, men and women of assorted nationalities. "We're our own United Nations," says Caplan, who works from dawn to dark six days a week—and thrives on it.

The Factors of Success

1. She perceived that there was a need to be filled: with canned mushrooms from Taiwan no longer available, fresh mushrooms were the answer.
2. She chose the name of her business shrewdly. She didn't use the word *gourmet* because people associate that with high prices.
3. She understood that promotion and public relations are especially important tools in building her type of business. She circularizes food editors with pictures, articcles, and recipes of each of her new products.
4. She educates produce managers and consumers with point-of-purchase posters, recipes, and instructions.
5. She doesn't rest on her laurels but is constantly on the lookout for new items. She introduces a new fruit or vegetable every six months.
6. She makes sure her products arrive at their destinations in top shape. She was a pioneer in shipping by air.
7. Her marketing strategy is shrewd. She prices her new products at forty-nine to fifty-nine cents a package, reasoning that "any woman will spend that much to make a meal more interesting."

East Side Partners

Their Business Is . . . a Restaurant

Among them, the six partners who run Summerhouse, an enchanting, plant-filled restaurant on Manhattan's upper East Side, have five husbands, twenty children, and two grandchildren. Dina Schmidt, Cynthia Walsh, and Susan McAllister are New Yorkers; Eloise O'Connell, June Jenkins, and Angelique Graxiano are Texans. They opened the restaurant because, "except for a hamburger joint and a few dingy holes in the wall, there was no place to eat in the neighborhood."

The most amazing part of their success is that they're now even better friends than they were before. Each invested $6,000, and though they started to make money from the beginning— "there was a line outside that went around the block the day we opened"—nobody drew a penny during the first year. "We plowed it all back in the business. We started with a home-sized fridge and a lot of make-do equipment from our various kitchens. As we made money, we invested in really professional kitchen equipment."

Summerhouse has a very special, very personal signature. The eye-catching carousel horse in the north window came from the home of one of the partners. The quaint little straight-backed chairs were picked up in the Hamptons and on the Bowery. Flowered chintz seats match the napkins that stand at attention in graceful balloon glasses. There are plants everywhere, fresh flowers on the tables.

The menu is also very personal. Among the entrées is a delight that *New York* magazine called "the best curried chicken salad in town." Fruited butters—strawberry, peach, or lemon— are always available. The pasta is freshly made, the desserts sinfully good. Cynthia's Cold Lemon Soufflé with fresh strawberries and Fantastic Fudge are sellouts. Prices are moderate. There is no bar, but customers are encouraged to bring their own wine.

Summerhouse started out with plenty of problems, endless emergencies. The contractors ruined the balcony floor, so, just hours before the opening, two of the partners got down on their hands and knees to sand and varnish. The contractors never told them they needed a grease trap under the sink. One was finally installed. But the contractors didn't tell them it had to be cleaned, so they were forced to have it emptied during lunch hour for an emergency fee. Two months after they opened, they discovered they didn't have a vital license. "We already had more than two dozen other licenses. If you want to learn about red tape and licenses, open a restaurant."

They got their first cook through a friend. He's still there. The waiters and waitresses—attractive young people with their eyes on Broadway—have been with them since the beginning. The partners have weathered all the storms and are busier and happier than they ever were before.

The Factors of Success

1. Because there are six people involved, "nobody is a slave to the business, and there's always somebody to take care of an emergency."

2. Their informal market research substantiated their initial hunch. The neighborhood they had their eye on has a dozen museums and as many private schools, providing a lucrative lunch trade. And the entire neighborhood drops in for dinner.

3. They use three purveyors each for meats, produce, fish. "That way we can always check on whether we're getting a fair price, and each supplier knows that if he wants to keep us as customers, he has to give top quality."

4. They divided their responsibilities efficiently. Four help in the kitchen, two specialize in keeping the books, all pinch-hit in the kitchen and as hostesses.

5. All the partners punch time clocks, just like the help. "That way, there's no question as to how much time each of us puts in."

6. There are no freebies. If husbands or children eat there, they get checks and pay—just like everybody else.

7. Their employees stay because the partners make it pleasant. Anyone who gets a chance to audition or a part in a play can take time off and come back when the play closes.
8. The restaurant always looks its best, and they're maniacal about keeping up the quality. "The food, the look, it's all important. If you're going to do it, you do it right. It's a matter of taste, of style."

Eva Brit Horton

Her Business Is . . . Importing Stoves

Ex-schoolteacher Eva Brit Horton is responsible for bringing wood stoves out of the backwoods camp and into the living room for the first time in fifty years. Founder and president of Kristia Associates in Portland, Maine, she's the exclusive importer of Norway's renowned wood-burning stoves.

It all began back in 1971, when she and her husband couldn't find a safe wood-burning stove to heat their country retreat in Maine. Remembering the wonderful wood-burning Jotul stoves of her Norwegian childhood and aware of the looming energy crisis, she put the two together and came up with an idea that motivated a trip to Norway the following year to arrange for an exclusive franchise to import Jotul stoves into the United States. The contract finally came through (it took a year to convince the manufacturer) on her fortieth birthday.

Horton marketed her stoves with considerable savvy, showing them first in art galleries to stress their elegant craftsmanship. She persuaded L. L. Bean, the Maine-based mail-order business, to put the stoves in its catalogue. She set up an organization of 600 dealers in thirty-seven states, crisscrossing the country to handpick them for their integrity and their belief in alternative energy sources. Dealers were also required to service the stoves they sold and conduct seminars she developed to teach the public how to get the most out of wood-burning stoves.

Her timing was perfect. Sales went from 5,000 units in 1974

to a projected 30,000 in 1981. Two years ago, Horton and Kristia Associates received an award from *Sales & Marketing Management* magazine for "outstanding sales and marketing achievement." The company was honored for recognizing "the nation's needs for alternative energy sources."

The Factors of Success

1. She recognized an opportunity.
2. She was persistent. It took her a year to get the Jotul franchise.
3. She is a born organizer. She had organized and run co-operative kindergartens and recreation centers in the past and even "ran her home like a business."
4. Working long hours didn't bother her.
5. She screened prospective dealers personally and chose them wisely.
6. She advertised widely and promoted her stoves like a pro. "Rekindle an old flame—HEAT WITH WOOD," "BURN WOOD and be a son of a birch," and "WOOD HEAT—Yours for the axing" are a few of the slogans on the bumper stickers and buttons she distributed.
7. She has diversified into quality iron cookware, also made by Jotul.

Iris Ellis

Her Business Is . . . Save on Shopping

It's a famous retail saying that "poor people need a bargain and rich people love one." Which accounts for the runaway success of *Save on Shopping,* a national directory of off-price outlet stores where one can buy top-quality, brand-name merchandise at a savings of 40 to 70 percent. Now in its eighth annual edition, the directory is the brainchild of Iris Ellis, whose nose for bargains has brought her fame, fortune, and more fan letters than a movie star.

Some ten years ago, Ellis's husband, head of the Dearborn, Michigan, Chamber of Commerce, asked her to take a group of visiting convention wives on a shopping tour. Ellis, who says it's against her religion to pay regular retail prices for anything, took the group to the outlet stores in the area, where the visitors stocked up on half-price-and-less Calvin Kleins and Pierre Cardins as if there were no tomorrow.

After several of these shopping expeditions, Ellis got the message. There were millions of potential bargain buffs across the country who needed only to be told where to hunt. "When I see something that needs to be done, I do it," she says.

Her directory, which now lists more than 7,000 stores, started out as a few typewritten pages stapled together. She offered it free to anyone who would send her the names of good bargain spots in other parts of the country. Either she or a trusted correspondent checked out each of the listings. "No discount shop with seconds or shoddy merchandise gets into *SOS*," states Ellis.

She started her business from her home, but when the mail began to pile up in her living and dining rooms and inundated the floor of her bedroom, she rented an office. Today she employs a secretary and an office manager and prints her own directory, which sells for $7.95. She crisscrosses the country checking out reputable bargain outlets and appears on TV in each city she visits to introduce women to bargain shopping with evangelical fervor.

Although she's helping to spark a retail revolution, she insists that "it's not me—the timing is perfect. Inflation has made everyone, even the rich, aware of the shrinking dollar. And today people don't want just a bargain; they want quality."

She tells her audiences that "*SOS* directory shopping will do more for your families than a big raise. The government taxes much of your raise year in and year out—but it doesn't tax away your bargain purchases."

The nation's 10,000 off-price stores accounted for $3 billion in sales in 1979, and that's only the beginning, prophesies Ellis, who's acting as consultant to developers of a new breed of off-price shopping malls and has plans for forming an association of off-price retailers. "Off-price shopping is not only here to stay—it's going to give conventional retailers a run for their money," she says. *SOS* is helping to make it happen.

The Factors of Success

1. She had an idea whose time had come and correctly perceived it as a genuine business opportunity.
2. She started the service from her home (rent free) and waited until it grew to rent an office.
3. She hired competent help.
4. She's a stickler for quality. Ellis checks out the merchandise in stores she recommends, examining fabrics, linings, buttonholes, and, in the case of appliances, warranties.
5. If she receives a complaint concerning a listing in her book, she investigates. If it's valid, the store is dropped from her directory.
6. She's a real publicity pro. She does all her own booking on television and makes her own press contacts.
7. She's a tireless ball of energy.

Carol Boyle

Her Business Is . . . Wind-N-Sun Shield Draperies

The energy crunch also provided Carol Boyle of Melbourne, Florida, with a golden opportunity. Carol, who had studied architecture and design, took out a $25,000 bank loan to set up a drapery and design studio. Why draperies? "Because," she explains, "they're one of the things that had to be custom-made for my clients, and instead of going elsewhere to have them made, I could do it on my own premises."

Her business was progressing at a slow and steady pace until she read about the heat-radiant vinyl laminate fabric being used in the Apollo moon missions. In a time of rising fuel costs, the words *heat radiant* struck a chord, and she decided to investigate. She drove down to Cape Canaveral, inspected the fabric, and went to work adapting it to home use. Eventually she designed and patented the Wind-N-Sun Shield system, which features a special rod that allows it to be hung with existing draperies to create an insulating—and money-saving—effect.

Press releases with photos were sent to about forty magazines. The resultant publicity produced a bumper crop of orders. "Suddenly," Boyle recalls, "I was in the mail-order business." Beefing up her staff of drapery-making seamstresses, she set about filling the orders and, thanks to the volume, was able to reduce the cost of the Wind-N-Sun Shield from $17.98 to a more affordable $9.00. This brought her an even greater volume of business. She's now expanding her business and has designed an entire home equipped with energy-efficient products.

Her spin-off from the space industry nets sales of over $200,000 a year from mail orders and earned her a nomination from the NASA magazine for "innovation in design and development." Entrepreneur Boyle not only has built a highly lucrative business but also has proved that moon missions can have warming fringe benefits.

The Factors of Success

1. She was innovative in her approach to her existing design company. The drapery workshop, which provided her clients with a needed service, also added to her profitability.
2. She was alert to the possibilities of the heat-radiant fabric.
3. She patented her design—the clue to preventing others from copying it.
4. She didn't hide her talent under a barrel. She publicized her product, sending photos and press releases to key publications.

5. She was prepared for volume—she already had a workshop and staff.

6. She reduced the price of her product to make it more attractive—and more affordable—to a greater number of people.

Jeanette Martin

Her Business Is . . . Merle Norman Cosmetic Studios

Back in 1965, ambitious, spunky Jeanette Martin, recently divorced and the mother of a little girl, went to work as a beauty adviser in a Merle Norman studio in Mobile, Alabama. "Other people hate to get up and go to work; I couldn't wait," she says. And she got a tremendous charge out of showing women how to look their best. "I loved it when they'd come back and tell me what their boyfriend or husband said."

After several years she began to yearn for a studio of her own, and when one came up for sale she borrowed $5,000 ("I had to go to three banks") and bought it. "It was terribly rundown, but I knew I could turn it around," she remembers. The studio was in downtown Mobile. Martin canvassed every office building in the vicinity, floor by floor, and invited the secretaries to her shop for free demonstrations. They came, they saw the miraculous change in the mirror—and they came back.

During the first six months she drew nothing out of her business, reinvesting the profits in inventory and improving the studio. By the end of the year, the business that had been going steadily downhill under the previous owner had grossed $100,000.

She heard of another studio for sale—in New Orleans—went up to look at it, got another bank loan—this one for $20,000—and bought it. That was in April 1971. By November she had bought another. In less than two years she had four Merle Norman studios in New Orleans, each in a prosperous shopping mall, and had sold the shop in downtown Mobile.

Two or three nights every week, after a long day's work, she would go out and speak to groups—the local garden club, a banking group, nurses, teachers. Wherever women gathered, Martin could be counted on to deliver a talk about the importance of grooming and appearance. At the end of each session she'd give a demonstration—a "make-over." The make-overs brought her many new customers. When women saw the change that artfully applied cosmetics could create, they came to her studios to learn the technique.

Today Martin has a manager and a staff of four or five salespersons in each of her studios. Last year the four shops grossed over $1 million.

The Factors of Success

1. Before she bought her first Merle Norman studio, Martin had worked in one for almost five years and knew the business.
2. She also knew the company well and says she chose Merle Norman because she realized how much help and support she would get. She received advice on choice of sites, and Merle Norman attorneys reviewed her leases. The company accountant advised on management.
3. She left Mobile and went to New Orleans, "where the grass was greener" and where, she believed, there were more opportunities.
4. She had a built-in sense of public relations. The canvassing of the office buildings, the talks to groups, the make-over demonstrations—all helped her build a large and loyal clientele.
5. She chose her employees carefully. One of her managers, a former schoolteacher, now makes double her previous salary. Three other managers had worked for other cosmetic companies and knew the business. All came as the result of personal recommendations.
6. Martin still gets a charge out of improving women's looks. It makes her feel "creative."

Barbara and Robert Kulicke

Their Business Is . . . Frames

Barbara and Robert Kulicke met at art school. Because many of their friends were artists, they were aware of the need for a new kind of picture frame, one that would give the work of art breathing space. "Our friends were looking for something other than wormy chestnut and gold leaf. They wanted understated frames in a new idiom, in materials like metal and plastic, relevant to modern architecture."

The Kulickes decided that making contemporary frames might have the potential of a good business and would be one very much related to their own interests. In 1950, with an investment of $1,000, they opened their first framing shop in a cold-water flat in New York. Each of the small rooms in the railroad flat served a different purpose—woodworking, mat making, fitting, finishing. Artists came and ordered frames, galleries became customers, and soon owners of contemporary art, attracted by the Kulicke's sparse and minimal framing, followed in growing numbers.

."But we were broke for a long time," says Barbara Kulicke, "because whatever money we made had to be put back into inventory." When the business outgrew the cold-water flat, the Kulickes borrowed the necessary capital from their families and moved to more spacious quarters. By then they had acquired a manufacturing facility in a lower Manhattan loft and 100 employees. The Kulicke Design Group created a series of frames that became contemporary classics. The welded aluminum frame and the clear-plastic do-it-yourself frames in a variety of sizes are international best sellers.

Along the way, Robert and Barbara Kulicke were divorced, and Robert left the business to go back to painting. Barbara stayed. Several years ago, Kulicke Frames was bought by a conglomerate. Recently Barbara took a leave of absence to write a book on the history of frames. "Frames tell the story of design from period to period," she points out.

The Factors of Success

1. The Kulickes chose a business they understood. They were art oriented and brought to their framing enterprise an intuitive understanding of how to frame a work of art—whether a painting, a graphic, or a poster—to its best advantage.
2. They had a nucleus of customers in their artist friends. Through the artists came the galleries.
3. Publicity in major architectural and interior design publications brought them to the attention of art collectors.
4. "We struggled more than we needed," reveals Barbara Kulicke, "because neither my husband nor I was a business person. We had no understanding of finance and the amount of record keeping required by the government. The ideal partnership is one in which one of the partners is the idea person, the other the financial brains. Had ours been that kind of partnership, it would have saved us innumerable headaches along the way and made us successful sooner."

Betty Owen

Her Business Is . . . a Secretarial School

Betty Owen was a midstream switcher. Fresh from college, she came to New York and landed a job as secretary to the fashion editor of *Vogue* magazine. She hoped to make it big in the fashion world, but after a stint on Seventh Avenue her enthusiasm waned. She then went to work for Booz, Allen and Hamilton, management consultants, as supervisor of secretarial services. There she became aware of the continual turnover of poorly trained secretaries, and it was there, she thinks, that the idea for her business was born.

But it was not until later, when she became assistant to a man who was starting a trade magazine, that the own-your-own-business bug really bit her. "I had a chance to see what goes into it—the market research, the advertising and direct mail, the promotion, the infinite detail and work that it takes to start a new enterprise."

From her experience at Booz, Allen and Hamilton, Owen knew that capable secretaries were difficult to come by. She decided that there was a place in the world—possibly a profitable place—for a school that could turn out well-trained, competent people. In 1965 she borrowed $5,000 and found suitable space. Since then she's moved four times, always to larger quarters.

Owen, with no intention of copying existing schools, had a definite concept of the kind of school she wanted to run: one that would teach students in small groups, with individual, personalized instruction; one with flexible programs in which students could learn at their own pace. The approach to teaching at Owen's secretarial school is progressive. Students learn with the aid of television and other electronic devices. The results: learning becomes an enjoyable—and speedier—experience.

She used direct mail from the beginning, continues to circularize graduating classes of schools as well as corporations, and recently added TV spots to her promotional arsenal. She now trains 2,000 people a year, from beginners to executives. She provides in-house instruction for corporations, supplies typing courses to many New York prep schools, and is currently expanding her curriculum to include communication skills.

In the seventeen years since she opened her school, she's come a long way financially. But her business has been rewarding in other ways as well. "Making my school grow," she explains, "forces me to expand my horizons and grow, too."

The Factors of Success

1. As a result of her job experience, she had a solid knowledge of her business.
2. She was creative about the kind of school she wanted to open.
3. Her fashion background and her own taste produced a school that was attractive, with space broken up into

small study rooms, bright graphics—a stimulating and attractive environment.

4. She understood the importance of advertising and promotion and continues to put a fixed percentage of her gross into them.

5. She hires people with top skills.

Lore Moser

Her Business Is . . . Parties

Lore Moser belongs in the *Guinness Book of World Records* as the woman who's given the most parties, "even more than Perle Mesta," she says. A graduate of the Cornell Hotel School, she was for many years banquet manager of Tavern-on-the-Green, the prestigious restaurant in New York's Central Park, where she masterminded more than 20,000 parties. This included composing the menu, selecting wines and flowers, designing decor—the works. "It got so that when somebody walked into my office, I could tell before a word was spoken whether the menu was to be roast beef and potatoes or guinea hen *sous cloche*."

Then, suddenly, the Tavern changed hands and closed for renovation for an indefinite period. "It was the first time in twenty years I'd had time to catch my breath," describes Moser. She decided, in spite of the flattering offers that came to her, that she really didn't want another job. She wanted to be on her own, in a business of her own. The solution? She became a party consultant, and for the past five years, working out of a sun- and plant-filled office in her apartment, Moser has continued to give one fabulous party after another.

For starters, she wrote to all the clients she had worked with at the Tavern, offering her services on a free-lance basis. Many responded, and many more have been added since. They range from the mother of the bride who wanted a sit-down champagne dinner for 200 with camellia bushes on every table to the Mobil Corporation, whose buffet for 600 in the Lincoln Center library to introduce the "Edward the King" television series featured oysters, smoked salmon, pâtés *en croûte,* chicken curry, roast suckling pig, trifles, tarts, pudding, and fruit in true Edwardian style. Moser's service is free to clients. Her fee comes from the restaurant or hotel where the party is given. If it's a catered party in a home, executive suite, or other private location, the catering service she employs pays her a commission. For the client, of course, it's sheer heaven. Under Moser's vigilant eye, nothing goes wrong. Strawberries and melons are ripe, steak is rare, wine chilled, service perfect. Moser has access to spectacular private homes and lofts that she uses for parties at which a special ambience is wanted. And she leaves nothing to chance. On an evening when she's giving parties for several clients, she taxis from one to the other to be sure everything is running smoothly, seeing to it that the hosts enjoy their parties as much as the guests do.

The Factors of Success

1. She was thoroughly familiar with her business.
2. She had a nucleus of potential clients.
3. She knew—and was known by—most of the top restaurant and hotel people in the city.
4. She is a connoisseur of food and wine.
5. She handles people—both clients and restaurant staffs—with tact, courtesy, and unfailing patience.
6. She's in a service business, and she provides service without stint.

Gloria Zigner

Her Business Is . . . Public Relations

Gloria Zigner came to be president and owner of a public-relations agency in Newport Beach, California, by a circuitous route—ready-to-wear, accounts receivable, a little theater group, and tennis. As a young woman out of college, she worked for her father in a clothing house, then for her husband in an accounts-receivable firm. As a result of the successful volunteer public-relations work she did for a little theater group, the city manager of Bakersfield hired her as consultant to the city.

Subsequently the Kern County Inter-Agency Council on Smoking and Health asked her to take on a two-year project: an antismoking campaign in the local high schools. Says Zigner, "I decided the best way to do it was to get the kids involved." She organized a group of students into an advertising and public-relations agency and had them create the no-smoking campaign. They came up with the Smoke, Choke, Croak slogan and under her supervision turned out a series of knockout ads and features that attracted national attention.

When soon thereafter Zigner, her husband, and her two sons moved to Newport Beach, where they knew nobody and she had no contacts, it didn't faze her. "Those were not," she points out, "very auspicious conditions in which to open an agency," but through one of her husband's tennis partners, Mrs. John Wayne, she was invited to handle a benefit for orphaned and homeless Peruvian children. The benefit was a smashing success. "How could it not be," asks Zigner, "with John Wayne as the celebrity guest?"

When a real-estate company hired her to help sell houses in a development, the tennis courts on the grounds sparked an idea in her fertile brain. She invited the tennis team from the University of California, Irvine, to beat the longest tennis match in the *Guinness Book of World Records,* promising a dollar for every spectator. Result: The University of California team beat the record, she contributed $2,000 to the tennis fund, and the real-estate development sold houses.

As her client list grew, she stopped being a one-woman agency. Today, with a staff of thirteen, Gloria Zigner Associates grosses well over $1 million a year. Among her clients: a number of financial institutions, hotels, restaurants, publishers. She handles many special events and recently acquired a West German manufacturer of videotapes as a client. "I pitched it for more than a year. I invited one of the vice presidents to a couple of special events. He was impressed, and we got the account."

The Factors of Success

1. She's a go-getter, a gregarious, extroverted woman who has a great gift for getting along with people.
2. With her inexhaustible store of energy, she can go all day *and* all night.
3. She is an enormously creative, one-woman brainstorming team with an idea a minute.
4. She knows how to implement a good idea and follow through down to the smallest detail.
5. She has an insatiable appetite for learning and continues to attend seminars and take courses.
6. She founded a women's networking group in Orange County, California, which meets once a month to pool information and ideas. It has been a fertile source of contacts—and of business.
7. She chooses her employees carefully, delegates responsibility, and rewards achievement.

Judith Haber and Evelyne Jankowski

Their Business Is . . . Chez Des Amis ("In the Home of Friends")

Until seven years ago when she and her husband were divorced, Judith Haber had never held a job. Evelyne Jankowski, recently arrived from her native France, was teaching French literature at Sarah Lawrence College. The two met, and from this unlikely pair, with not an ounce of previous business experience between them, came an idea that's making ripples in the travel business and will soon be making even bigger waves.

Chez Des Amis makes it possible for American tourists going abroad to lodge in attractive, well-appointed homes with a gracious host and hostess. "Instead of staying in an impersonal hotel where they're a room number," says Haber, "they can visit a picturesque manor, a farmhouse, or even a castle and meet people who will see to it that they thoroughly enjoy their stay."

They started small. Jankowski, who has friends and relatives in France, spent a summer traveling from one end of the country to the other, searching out likely prospects. It wasn't easy. She met resistance from many of the French, who initially thought that Americans were barbarians but have since been charmed and delighted by their guests. She came back with twenty-five host families signed up. After the partners notified the travel section of the *New York Times* concerning the availability of private homes in different areas of France through Chez Des Amis, the *Times* ran a two-paragraph story about it, and "the phone never stopped ringing," says Haber. "In less than a month we had 5,000 inquiries."

The first summer Chez Des Amis placed 100 clients in host homes and made a modest profit. By the third year they were able to buy the brownstone from which they were running their business. Now in their seventh year, they have seventy carefully researched host families throughout France, sixty in the British Isles, an office in Paris, and a clientele of many thousands. A 318-page catalogue describes each of the host homes in detail: accommodations, facilities for children, surrounding area, availability of meals, costs.

Haber and Jankowski spend two months a year visiting the various host homes and lining up new ones. Their plans for the future include setting up a network of available homes in other countries and arranging for host homes in the United States for travelers from abroad. In just seven short years, an idea for which there was a need has burgeoned into a profitable business with limitless horizons.

The Factors of Success

1. They had a new idea in travel, one that had not occurred to the nearly 18,000 travel agents in the United States.
2. They worked hard, often around the clock, to make their idea a reality.
3. In the beginning, they often spent two to three hours with a prospective client to be sure of signing him or her

up with the right host family. This year they produced a catalogue with detailed descriptions of the host homes, families, and available facilities so that clients can intelligently make their own choices.

4. They also started by making the travel arrangements for their clients, but now they work through a worldwide computerized travel service with an 800 telephone number that clients can call directly. This has eliminated the need for two employees and freed the partners to concentrate on future planning.

5. From the beginning they were aware of the value of publicity and advertising and were in constant contact with travel editors. They advertised consistently.

6. Their service is reliable; most homes are carefully checked out to be sure that the clients sent there will have an enjoyable experience. Many like it so much they return for a second stay.

What Lessons Can Be Drawn?

There are common denominators in the success stories of the women we've described here. In fact, they are many of the necessary ingredients that account for the success of every woman whose business survives and thrives.

The most prevalent thread running through each of their stories is the love these entrepreneurs have for what they are doing. They all claim it is this enthusiasm that fuels the commitment of long hours and hard work.

They describe support systems, encouraging and helpful husbands if they are married, children who pitch in, friends who provide relief from the long hours of toil or who actually participate in making the business a success, lawyers, accountants, and others who have acted as trusted advisers.

These women took special care in the selection of their employees and understood that marketing and promotion—letting the world know what they had to offer—were as important as the quality of the product or service itself.

Most, but not all, knew their businesses before they began, a fact that obviously gave them a good head start. Though none of the partners in Summerhouse had ever owned a restaurant, they were all excellent cooks and constant diners-out. They also had an unerring sense of where such an establishment could succeed.

A number of the women—Scurry of Wicker Garden, Horton of Kristia Associates, Owen with her secretarial school, and Caplan of Produce Specialties—diversified by developing other product lines or identifying new markets for their services and thus increased the profitability of their businesses.

In addition, a number of these women had original and rather unique ideas, although some did not. In fact, most small businesses that are successful are not the first or the only ones in their fields. A well-managed enterprise that offers something that the public is aware of, wants, and can afford is clearly the key.

Most important, however, these women saw themselves as creators, organizers, and learners—classic qualities of the successful entrepreneur. They didn't count hours or watch the clock, nor did they give up easily when confronted with difficulties. On the contrary: they perceived these difficulties as challenges to be overcome.

Despite the difficulties, there are few satisfactions that rival becoming a successful entrepreneur. The chapters that follow outline in more detail the skills, tools, and methods—the professional and personal strategies—that can make you an economically independent woman.

CHAPTER 2

There's No Business Like Small Business

I f you think small business is small, think again. Of the more than thirteen million American businesses that file tax returns each year, 97 percent are small, local, family, and independent enterprises. What's more, those thirteen million small businesses provide fully 55 percent of all private employment in the country, 50 percent of all business activity, and 43 percent of the gross national product.

What *has* been small—at least until recently—is the number of women who are participating in the satisfactions and rewards of owning a business of their own. According to figures compiled by the Small Business Administration (SBA), women, who comprise more than 50 percent of the population, owned only 7.1 percent of U.S. businesses in 1980.

Think about those numbers and the ones that follow—they speak louder than a thousand words:

Of the forty-four million women who work outside the home, according to 1978 figures, only 6 percent earn between $15,000 and $25,000 a year. Six times that many men, however, are in that salary range.

Almost 80 percent of the women who work are in sales, clerical, or light factory jobs. Men, on the other hand, hold about 78 percent of all managerial jobs.

Less than 0.8 percent of working women earn $25,000 a year.

The average working woman earns $8,618 a year, while the average salary for men is $14,006 a year.

Is it any wonder, then, that intelligent, capable, ambitious women of all ages and in all parts of the country are turning to entrepreneurship, starting businesses of their own as a means of achieving economic independence? Again, the numbers tell the story: In 1979, 800,000 women owned their own businesses, double the number of 400,000 in 1972.

It was bound to happen. As we shed the old stereotypes, as we became better educated, more confident, and more ambitious, as more and more of us became heads of households, it was inevitable that women would discover the satisfactions and financial rewards that come with owning and operating one's own enterprise.

What Is a Small Business?

The small-business umbrella shelters a tremendous variety of enterprises. The neighborhood cleaner, a public-relations firm that specializes in politics, your favorite restaurant, a registry of practical nurses, and the manufacturer of custom gift boxes can all call themselves small businesses. The general description that follows indicates just how broad the boundaries of the category are.

A small business is usually an independently owned operation, not dominant in its field, that manufactures or sells a product or provides a service to the consumer or to other business concerns. The majority of small businesses are sole proprietorships, (that is, owned by one individual). Others are partnerships, and many are also corporations, a type of business structure that has certain tax and personal advantages. Almost always they are owner operated, meaning that the owner or owners are active in all phases of the day-to-day operation.

It's difficult to define a small business in terms of annual sales volume or number of employees. According to the SBA, a retail business can have a gross income ranging from $100,000 to $2 million a year and still be considered a small business. For a small wholesale business, the annual sales could be $9.5 million!

A small business typically occupies a single location (though it may occupy several) and on a national average employs up to 4 persons—but a manufacturing business with as many as 200 employees is also considered within this category. A small business can be located anywhere: downtown, in a neighborhood shopping center, out on a highway, in an office building, even in your own home.

Getting Started

Instead of starting your business from scratch, you may want to buy one that's already established. The best place to look for a business for sale is in your local newspaper under Business Opportunities. Real-estate agents, accountants, bankers, and lawyers are also excellent sources of information on businesses for sale. If you have some special interest—pets, flowers, jewelry, crafts—trade associations and business brokers can often help you locate a business related to your field.

Even when you find what you think may be the perfect business for sale, be wary. Investigate. Find out why it's for sale. Is the present owner retiring, or is the business going downhill and does the owner want out? Sometimes a business that's losing money because of poor management can be turned around with good management. Buying a poorly run but promising firm at a bargain price can be a very profitable way to go into business

In deciding how much to pay for a going business, you should consider its profitability, tangible assets, certain intangibles, and liabilities. Study authentic records of the business over a period of years. Some businesses may have inadequate records, but all should have copies of income-tax returns. Are the profits satisfactory? If not, what are the chances of improving them?

Evaluate the physical facilities as well. Are the premises attractive? What are the lease arrangements? Is the neighborhood a good one, or is it run-down, a potential candidate for urban razing a few years hence? Find out what government agencies have jurisdiction over the business and whether there have ever been any violations of federal and state laws.

Before you make any offer, have an accountant go over the records and guide you on your offering price. Once you and the seller agree on a price, you will want your attorney to draw up a contract that will protect you. Among other things, a favorable contract will give you clear title, good payment terms, and warranty protection against false statements by the seller.

You May Want to Investigate Franchises

A franchise is an individually owned business operated as though it were part of a large chain. H & R Block and McDonald's are examples. There are also some new twists in franchises—exercise studios and career-counseling centers, among others.

If you're eager to go into a business of your own but dread the hassle of getting started, a franchise may be the perfect solution. A well-known name on a shop front can be an enormous asset. For a fee, the supplier (franchiser) gives you the right to use the name and sell the product or service. The franchise agreement generally requires you to purchase your supplies and equipment from the franchiser, and you may have to pay a percentage of your gross sales.

One fringe benefit to owning a franchise is that the cash outlay for buying one is often lower than what you'd need to set up a business of your own. Moreover, it may even be easier to get a bank loan to purchase a franchise than to get one start your own business.

If you decide that a franchise is for you, make sure the one you choose fits you. It should be in a field that appeals to you, something that you're good at. Your franchise should involve you with the kind of people you like, and it should also offer a service or product that fills a need in your community.

Take the time to investigate the parent company. If it's publicly owned, get a copy of its annual report. Telephone or write for information regarding what the company offers in the way of a franchise package. Does it provide any substantial assistance? Will it help you find a location, assist in the design of your shop, train you? Does it offer a continuing educational program?

Do your own market research. Visit at least one of the franchises near you. Really study it—see what sort of people patronize it, how busy it is, how well or poorly it is run. Interview the owner. Go back several times. Talk to the customers. Find out what they think of the parent company and its products

Before you invest your money or give up the security of working for somebody else, scrutinize the business philosophy of the franchising company. Ask yourself these questions:

1. How long has it been in business?
2. Has it changed its goals in the last few years?
3. Does its thinking coincide with yours?

A good partnership strengthens you and multiplies your potential. Merle Norman Cosmetics, the company we know best, has been in business for fifty years with the same philosophy, the same goals. To help their studio owners succeed, the company makes available to its applicants the services of its real-estate department. A location counselor not only assists in finding and evaluating a site but offers help in negotiating the rental structure, and the company's legal department reviews all proposed leases.

Ninety-nine percent of the more than 2500 privately owned, non-franchised Merle Norman studios in the United States and Canada are owned by women, many of whom have several studios and gross more than $1 million a year. This is as much testament to the entrepreneurial capacity of these women as it is to the quality of support they receive.

To repeat: Know the company, know the product or products it sells. Do your own market research to find out how customers feel about the product and the parent company.

Now, what kind of woman does it take to succeed in her own small business?

It Takes an Entrepreneur

Entrepreneur is a word you'll come across often in this book. It's defined as someone who undertakes a business, someone who organizes, manages, and assumes the risk of a business enterprise Note: The key words here are *assumes the risk*. No matter what business you choose to go into, there's never a guarantee of success. The mortality rate of small businesses is very high: 50 percent fail in the first two years. That's why, before you begin, it's essential for you to understand the factors that may make the difference between success and failure. They are—not necessarily in this order—

1. The right idea at the right time and in the right place
2. Money
3. The desire to succeed
4. Determination
5. Vision
6. Expertise in a particular field
7. Resourcefulness
8. A desire to learn
9. Organizational ability
10. Time

The owner of a small business has to be a Jill-of-all-trades, able to attract and hold customers, repair the typewriter, read a profit-and-loss statement, sweep the floor, deal with suppliers and landlords and employees, keep her cool, her health, her sense of humor, and her head.

You Need Drive—Lots of It

If you want to go into business for yourself, first and foremost you need the drive and the will to work harder than you ever believed possible. This may not be as burdensome as it sounds, though. The women we interviewed for this book say that working for themselves feels different from working for others—no matter how many hours they put in, there is rarely any sense of resentment. In fact, their major complaint is that the day doesn't have more hours.

You also need individuality, flair, and creativity to make you different from and better than your competition. You need the cooperation of your family and close friends, because when you work long hours you'll have less time for them. Unless they understand this and are 100 percent behind you, you'll have problems.

Everybody who goes into business wants to succeed; but there's a vast, yawning chasm between wanting and doing. This book is intended to narrow that gap. We want to demystify the process of starting and running a business and to encourage women who believe they have the initiative, motivation, and ability it takes to be successful at it.

In many ways, small business is the seed bed of our national economy. New ideas and innovative products are very often introduced by small companies. More than 50 percent of the new products introduced every year come from small businesses.

Individuals with a need to achieve, a high risk and a low frustration tolerance, a desire for independence, and an impatience with routine are the most likely candidates for becoming entrepreneurs. Men and women who want to make more money than they can make working for somebody else see in small business their best chance to strike it rich.

Success in a business of your own brings not only economic but personal rewards as well. A business of your own gives you the best of all worlds—a career, independence, and the indefinable joy of self-fulfillment. Going into business can be one of the most exciting and satisfying steps you'll ever take.

There are many advantages in being small. Since you're not bound by tradition, you can follow up on a new idea and not be held down by the slow and methodical ways of big organizations. There's no bigger thrill than being able to run a risk, to take a long shot and come out on top. As anyone who's ever done it before will testify, creating a business of your own may turn out to be the greatest adventure of your life.

CHAPTER 3

Are You Ready to Start at the Top?

t's nice to be your own boss and start at the top. The fact is, however, that hardly anybody does. In one way or another, those who succeed in a small business have prepared for it. They have what it takes in terms of practical on-the-job training, volunteer experience, education, psychological and physical stamina, financial and managerial know-how, and more. They are, in essence, ready to succeed.

Your choice of business, of course, is a key ingredient in the recipe for success. But even more important is your knowledge of how the product or service you plan to sell relates to the general consumer climate and whether it represents a *genuine business opportunity*.

How do you recognize a genuine business opportunity? It goes without saying that an idea—a good idea—is of paramount importance. It should be an idea for a product or service that fills a real need—for example, the fast-food restaurants that have proliferated because now a large percentage of women are in the work force and at the end of the day they have neither the time nor the inclination to cook. Or the self-defense schools and home security services that are doing brisk business in urban and suburban areas with climbing crime rates. Or the car-rental companies that provide executives and tourists with instant wheels. Or the matchmaking services, computerized and personal, that find compatible partners for singles. Or the shopping services geared to pressed-for-time working women and men.

But a need alone isn't enough. It has to exist in sufficient volume so that the product or service can be marketed at a price that produces a profit. This is the essence of the genuine business opportunity.

Discovering the Genuine Business Opportunity

There are a number of ways to identify the genuine business opportunity. The most usual is to latch onto an expanding market for an existing product or service that can support additional businesses of the same type. Hertz was followed by Avis, McDonald's by Burger King. The market for many products and services is big enough to support lively competition.

Another situation that presents a valid opportunity for a new business is one in which the need for a product or service is not being adequately met by existing firms.

A third opportunity exists in the introduction of a new product or service that's targeted to the needs of a large enough segment of the market to generate sufficient sales and produce a profit. The inexpensive pocket calculator is a dramatic example of this type of opportunity.

Spotting the Trends

Certain social and economic factors help create genuine opportunities for the small-business entrepreneur. An examination of trends during the past decade provides some revealing hints.

During the 1970s we experienced unprecedented affluence. More people than ever before had more to spend, the time to spend it, and the credit available when they didn't have ready cash. As a result, the demand for luxury items and services increased. This accounts for the rapid growth of a large variety of specialty shops—businesses specializing in fashion, books, records, decorative objects for the home, gourmet appliances, games, musical instruments—that you now find routinely in many shopping centers.

More disposable income resulted in a dramatic increase in dollars spent for recreation and repair services. Ski shops, bicycle stores, and hobby shops mushroomed. As the number of truly wealthy people increased, so did the yacht dealerships, travel agencies, caterers, and other purveyors of "the good life."

The last decade also spawned antimaterialist and counter-culture trends. One badge of the counterculture was to wear worn-out, shabby clothing. A. E. Morris saw this as a genuine business opportunity and created a successful business by man-ufacturing new jeans that looked like old ones!

Increasing awareness of health, the new-found popularity of physical activities like jogging, the cult of natural foods—natural everything—presented genuine business opportunities. Joggers needed special shoes and clothing. Health-food freaks went for yogurt, pumpkin seeds, sprouts, tofu, and anything organically grown. Fitness-conscious men and women were ready-made patrons for well-equipped gyms.

The cultural explosion created a demand for books, arti-facts, graphics, posters, antiques, and reproductions of works of art. Nelson Rockefeller saw that as a genuine business op-portunity and set up a shop that sold reproductions of his own famous art collection. Dwindling living space in Manhattan sug-gested a profitable business to a young woman who had accu-mulated a nest egg importing rugs from Turkey. With two part-ners, bought she searched for a warehouse in SoHo, bought a property, and converted it into luxury condominiums.

The changing roles of women have created an explosion of genuine business opportunities. Career workshops, assertive-ness training classes, return-to-work seminars, financial coun-seling magazines for working women, boutiques with fashions for career women, and shopping services are just a few from among hundreds. Working mothers' awareness of the dangers for latchkey children has resulted in a variety of afterschool options—creative play schools, enrichment programs for teenagers, services that provide surrogate mothers for a few hours in the afternoon.

The energy crisis led to a resurgence in the bicycle business and the beginnings of a solar industry. The greening of America blossomed into plant and gardening shops. The disco epidemic produced a new wave of fashions and dance emporiums. Now country western is in.

Some of the fads, fancies, and foibles of the seventies will continue into the eighties; many will disappear and be replaced by new ones, opening up a whole new horizon of business opportunities. But it's wise to remember that fads are risky. If you're going to put your money into a fad business, be sure to get in at the beginning because they sometimes fade fast, presenting more peril than promise.

The Consumer Climate

In zeroing in on genuine business opportunities, it's important to be aware of the consumer climate. Highly sophisticated research tools and techniques are employed to probe consumer tastes and forecast future trends by such companies as Lou Harris, Gallup, and Yankelovich. You can tap into this information by making it your business to read the *Wall Street Journal,* the business section of your local newspaper, and *Business Week* magazine; they are invaluable resources for every woman who wants to keep abreast of trends and directions and how they affect the economic climate.

What About the Eighties?

Two major segments of the consumer market that emerged in the seventies are still with us today. Most simply, they can be described as *self-fulfillment* and *personal experience* groups. Those in the self-fulfillment group put less emphasis on clothing and possessions, more on education, achievement, and quality of life. (If "self-fulfillers" jog, it's not because jogging is a fad but because they want to keep fit.) Those who fall into the personal-experience category, on the other hand, want sensation, change, novelty.

The consensus is that a recession, in and of itself, does not bring about major retrenchment. While households may downgrade from sirloin to chuck, those interested in the good things in life, who believe, "I deserve the best," will keep the luxury market booming in the eighties.

The growing phenomena of job sharing, flex-time, and four-day work weeks will create more leisure, making businesses that deal in sports, education, hobbies, culture, and entertainment prosper in the eighties. TV and the revolution of rising expectations have democratized aspirations and broadened the market for goods and services.

Even an economy in some trouble provides opportunities. As we go to the printer with this book, interest rates on home loans are at an all-time high—and so are profits in the home remodeling business. Instead of moving to larger houses, people are opting to enlarge their current dwellings.

We're also beginning to see the emergence of discount shopping malls where consumers can purchase the luxury goods to which they have become accustomed, but at the lowest possible prices.

As you research and evaluate business opportunities, keep the self-fulfillment and personal-experience groups in the foreground of your mind. And don't forget the working woman and her family. Weigh any genuine business opportunity against the interests of these groups. Anything that deals with self-improvement—physical, emotional, or career oriented—will be highly marketable.

It's also worth noting that the population as a whole is growing older. The businesses devoted to fitness and health are but one manifestation of this emerging market. The latest census figures provide a clue of a different sort. For the first time in this century, people are leaving cities and suburbs for small towns. This interesting phenomenon has already led to the emergence of some new businesses and will inevitably spawn more.

What's Right for you?

While genuine business opportunities may appear to be unlimited, your individual choice should be narrowed down to a business in which you have some background. Your own skills, experience, and knowledge ultimately determine which type of business opportunity is right for you. If you can't boil an egg and don't know fricassee from frittata, it would be foolhardy to open a shop that specializes in gourmet cooking accessories. If you can't distinguish a buck-and-wing from a waltz, you shouldn't consider opening a dancing school.

But even a bona fide genuine business opportunity will be only as good as the woman who grasps it. The prosperity of a business depends on the strengths, abilities, and motivations of the owner. The person you see when you look in the mirror will play the major role in determining the success—or failure—of your business.

What does it take to be a successful entrepreneur? Your answers to the questions that follow will tell you if you're ready to start at the top and what your chances are of staying there.

Why Do You Want to Go into a Business of Your Own?

1. You want to be your own boss.
2. A business of your own will give you more prestige.
3. You want a chance to express yourself.
4. You want to make money—lots of money.
5. Your children are grown, and you need something to occupy your time.

All the above reasons are valid. The entrepreneurs who have been most successful, however, have been motivated primarily by a desire to make money and to be self employed—to be their own boss.

Do You Have Experience?

If you're planning to open a fashion boutique, have you worked in a clothing or accessory shop or had department-store buying experience? These are the best ways to know the market, to learn the nitty-gritty of buying and reordering, to understand the psychology of the consumer—what turns her off, what turns her on—and to learn the dos and don'ts of the fashion business.

It's only common sense that you have a far better chance of succeeding in a business you know something about than in one with which you're unfamiliar. A copywriter in a major Chicago advertising agency decided to start a business of her own. She looked into a number of possible business openings but in the end decided to provide a copywriting service for smaller, understaffed agencies. Her company, Copy Cat, supplies copy, speeches, mailorder advertising, brochures, leaflets. She now has two full-time employees plus several free-lancers and is thinking of adding layout and art to her roster of services. The secret of her success: she knew her business.

If you don't know *your* business, learn it before you put your ego on the line and risk your capital. Want to open a catering service? Work in somebody else's before starting one from your home. Want to open a restaurant? First get a job in one.

Linda Jackson, who had ten years of experience as a bank loan officer, decided to go into her own business. She went to night school, earned a master's degree in business administration, and then hung out her own shingle as a management consultant. Now she helps her clients apply for bank loans and counsels them on managing their businesses—at a $300-per-diem fee.

Do You Know How to Mind Your Business?

At the beginning you probably won't be able to afford a full-time bookkeeper. Do you know how to keep records? Will you be able to tell at a glance whether you're making or losing money?

It's not necessary to be a Sylvia Porter with a background in economics and finance, but unless you have some knowledge of cash flow, profit and loss statements, sales projection, and inventory control, you run a high risk of instant failure.

Do you know what your taxes will be, what kind of insurance you'll need? Do you know how to keep and take care of an inventory? How to get the most out of your employees? Fortunately, there are courses that will give you a working knowledge of bookkeeping and business management.

Do You Have the Image of Success?

When you look in the mirror, do you see a well-groomed, put-together woman who looks successful? Are your clothes well tailored and well coordinated? Obviously, the nature of your business will make a difference in the way you dress. The woman who opens a trendy boutique will dress differently from the management consultant; neither will resemble the owner of a children's gymnastic studio. Specific occasions will also dictate what is appropriate. Even the most casually or exotically dressed woman will choose a conservative outfit when visiting a banker or speaking to the local Jaycees.

Successful women pay attention to their appearance. They are well groomed and look contemporary. To them, a super wash-and-wear haircut that lets them look their best day after day is as a necessity, not a luxury. They have also learned the subtleties of makeup and dress. If these are not your strong points, we advise getting some expert help. Give yourself the image of success. From the banker who considers your loan to prospective customers and clients, people measure you by the way you look.

Evaluate Yourself

In business you deal with many kinds of people, so your ability to get along with them will be a major factor in your success.

The ability to communicate persuasively and well with your clients, your banker, your landlord, your suppliers, your customers, and your employees is an indispensable skill.

Evaluate yourself realistically. Can you write a clear, concise, persuasive letter? Can you give precise, easy-to-understand-and-follow instructions and criticism to an employee? Are you a convincing, interesting speaker? How are you on the telephone? Have you had much practice in the art of negotiating? Are you good at selling?

Most people are strong in some of these areas and weak in others. If you feel you need to improve your communication skills, adult education courses at your local community college or university extension division can help you upgrade these vital assets. A course in public speaking will stand you in just as good stead on a one-to-one basis, and platform know-how will come in handy should you be asked to address a group or appear on a TV program.

A few more questions:

1. Are you a self-starter, or do you turn over for one more snooze after the alarm rings?
2. Are you an organizer, or do you sit back and wait for somebody else to take on the responsibility?
3. Do you need to follow somebody else's work structure, or can you create your own?
4. Do you like to work hard? Nobody works harder than the boss of her own business.
5. Are you the kind of person who gets bogged down in details, or can you delegate responsibility?
6. Have you ever worked for someone in a managerial capacity or been responsible for a major volunteer effort?
7. Can you balance your checkbook?
8. Do you make a budget and stick to it?
9. Are you in good health? Treasure and take care of it. Health and energy are major business assets.
10. Do you have confidence in yourself? This is a must, so if you don't have it, develop it fast. How? Make a list

of all the things you do well, whether it's giving a party, arranging flowers, taking Cub Scouts on outings, organizing a new filing system, or collecting funds for charity. From this moment on, make it a point to take on responsibilities, whether at home or at work. Keep a list of your successes and read it over frequently to build confidence in yourself.

11. Are you a risk taker? Most women are, though until recently these risks have been taken primarily on the domestic front. For example, any woman who has moved a family from one city to another and in the process built a new life has taken many risks.

To succeed in business, you need the qualities mentioned above, along with tact, friendliness, resourcefulness, assertiveness, and lots of enthusiasm. How do you rate yourself on these?

Most small-business failures are the result of poor planning and poor management. One could almost say that those who failed prepared to fail. The ones who succeeded are the ones who prepared for it and worked at it.

Remember the Broadway hit called *How to Succeed in Business Without Really Trying?* It may work on the stage but never in real life. The people who usually succeed in business are those who do like the car-rental company—they try harder!

CHAPTER 4

Lawyers, Accountants, Bankers, and Brokers

Your Basic Business Consultants

T he one thing a small-business owner can't afford is to *think* small. A business that plans for success will start out by securing the same professional services that a big business uses—an attorney, an accountant, an insurance broker, and often a banker as well. These are not luxuries but necessities without which you literally can't function.

The American business system is such a maze of regulations and laws, the tax structure so complicated, the IRS so ubiquitous, that trying to run a business without expert professional help is a folly. Large corporations hire such professionals as full-time employees. The small-business owner will buy this specialized help on a part-time fee basis.

In some cases it's obvious when you're in need of professional advice. If you're sued, you need a lawyer; for a financial statement or tax return, you turn to an accountant; if you need insurance coverage, you consult an insurance broker.

Fringe Benefit

Actually, these professional consultants can provide assistance on many other occasions. If you're lucky, you may even end up with a fringe benefit, because there's another role each of these pros can play in your business—that of general adviser. Each is familiar with the entire spectrum of business problems and the various ways of solving them.

In time you may find that you have better rapport with one of these professionals than you do with the others. Cultivate it. There's probably nothing more useful to a business owner than a chance to talk things over with an informed, objective outsider. Such informal exchanges often give you a better understanding of your own business, and sometimes just "shooting the breeze" gives birth to valuable ideas.

The Functions of an Attorney

As a small-business owner you're going to require legal help in many areas. At the outset, your most important decision will be the legal form your business will take. You have a number of options, and a lawyer can describe the advantages and disadvantages of each. Small businesses typically are sole proprietorships, partnerships, or corporations.

A *sole proprietorship* is run by one person or a husband and wife. Most of the thirteen million small businesses in the United States are sole proprietorships. In the sole proprietorship, the owner runs the business his or her way, makes all the decisions, exercises independent control. But the sole proprietor also has complete legal and financial responsibility. Any debt or obligations of the business are the personal responsibility of the owner. Creditors can attach his or her personal assets.

A *partnership* is often desirable because two persons—or three or four, as the case may be—bring more diversified skills, more ideas, and more capital into a business. The legal aspects are the same as in a sole proprietorship. Each of the partners is personally responsible for the debts and legal obligations of the business.

A *corporation*, on the other hand, is a totally different type of entity. A corporation has a legal existence of its own, and an incorporated business is legally separate from its owners. There are numerous advantages to this type of business structure. Your attorney can advise you about specific regulations in your state.

Note: There's a form of corporation known as *Subchapter S,* which is a cross between a traditional corporation and a partnership. While it has the same structure as a "normal" corporation and offers limited liability to the owners, a Sub S corporation pays no corporate income tax. Moreover, as in a partnership, the profits of the corporation go to the owners, who are taxed as individuals. This form is especially attractive to certain types of investors.

Most businesses start out as sole proprietorships; some incorporate after a couple of years. Your attorney can best advise you on what form your business should take.

Contracts and Leases

Starting one's own business inevitably leads to the signing of innumerable legal documents. Unless you own the building in which you are conducting your activities, you will probably have to sign a lease. You will be faced with contracts as well if you lease or purchase equipment, if you install a security system, or if you borrow money.

There may be contracts that are very specific to the kind of business you are running. These are often printed in what appears to be a standard form, as if every contract or lease of this sort has the same provisions, but don't automatically believe this. The persons who prepared the agreement have typically written it in a way that is more advantageous to them than to you. There is almost always some room for negotiation. A woman we know was able to convince one of the major corporations that provides copying machines to change its "standard" agreement.

Unless you are very sophisticated about contract language, your attorney's services can be very valuable here. He or she should review every important contract or lease to be signed.

The attorney can interpret all the ifs, ands, buts, and fine-print stipulations—and, in the process, he or she can educate you about contract language so that down the line you will be able to do more of this on your own. It's also valuable to be present when your attorney negotiates on your behalf, since again this presents an opportunity to learn. If you have the kind of business in which those who seek your services sign an agreement prepared by you, your attorney can assist or actually draw up this document.

Business Licenses

Your attorney will be aware of and can advise you concerning the licenses needed for your specific endeavor.

A local business license is required to open every enterprise. Some businesses must also conform to local zoning codes as well as fire and police regulations. These requirements are nothing to trifle with. If you don't have the correct permit or don't meet the building requirements, the police or fire department can shut you down.

Every state that collects a sales tax issues "sellers' permits," and every business that sells merchandise must have one. A firm that exports goods to foreign countries must also have a valid export license. In today's protect-the-consumer climate, many businesses, ranging from a marriage-counseling bureau to a dry-cleaning establishment, require licenses.

Insurance

Your attorney will advise you on the various kinds of insurance your business will need. He or she may also be able to recommend a good broker. It's also wise to have your attorney review the policies before you make final purchasing decisions.

Lawsuits: Winning and Avoiding

It's obvious that you need professional advice if you are sued or plan to institute a suit. But not enough is said about the role of attorneys in preventing such potentially messy, expensive, and unpleasant situations. It's wise to discuss your preferences in this regard with your attorney, since he or she can be helpful in avoiding problems and resolving conflicts before they reach the lawsuit stage.

Anyone with business experience will counsel you to talk to your attorney *before* you make any major moves—not after. To make the best use of your attorney, don't wait until you're in trouble for a consultation.

The Lawyer as Business Advisor

There was Amy Bennett with a toy shop—educational toys for upper-middle-class children in an affluent Chicago suburb—doing middling to moderately well. Her lawyer had just finished going over some contracts for her and lingered to chat. As they talked, his eye fell on several pieces of miniature doll-house furniture, which he picked up and admired.

Each had been exquisitely handcrafted by Amy's father-in-law, who was retired and made them as a hobby. The lawyer asked if they sold; Amy told him she couldn't keep them in stock. He suggested setting up a separate department for the miniatures. Today Amy no longer sells toys. She sells doll houses and miniature furniture to the tune of a six-figure annual gross. Her father-in-law, who built a studio behind his house, now has three full-time employees.

You won't find Business Advisers listed in the yellow pages, but you may find a lawyer, accountant, insurance broker, or banker who fills that slot. This is not something that happens overnight; it's a relationship that takes time to develop. Choose your professional advisers for their expertise and affordability, but try to develop that special relationship with at least one of them.

If that special person is your attorney, he or she may have useful suggestions when it comes to collectnhg debts owed to your company. Or advice about a disgruntled employee or angry customer. Or information on the structuring of a stock offering. A good lawyer will also show you how to take maximum advantage of tax laws. This list certainly isn't meant to be all-inclusive, merely to give you some idea of the ways your attorney (or accountant) can help.

Finding a Good Attorney

The best way to find a lawyer is through personal recommendations. Other entrepreneurs provide the best leads, since their problems and needs are similar to your own. Your accountant, insurance broker, or banker may also have suggestions. When you are given a name, probe for information. Other business owners should be able to describe difficult situations they have confronted with their attorneys and how they performed. Ask about the fees charged, the lawyer's abilities as a negotiator, his or her willingness and skill as a business adviser and connections with the financial community. If the person recommended is a male attorney, see if you can get a reading on his attitudes about women in business. The most skilled legal adviser will be very difficult to work with if he doesn't believe you belong where you are.

You don't need or want a big corporation or patent attorney. What you should look for instead is a generalist who has had experience in handling small businesses. While there are both pros and cons to using a family friend as your attorney, we recommend a straight professional relationship as the best arrangement.

Take the time to interview at least two or three candidates for the job. Take a draft of your business proposal and a list of questions prepared beforehand. It's at this initial meeting that you can determine what the fees will be, any potential conflicts of interest with other clients, and whom you'll work with if he or she is not available or if you run into an area of law outside this attorney's expertise. Here is an excellent opportunity to use your intuition. Do you like this person? Will you feel comfortable asking questions? Do you sense the attorney will have the time for you and a genuine interest in your becoming successful?

We advise accepting the fact that the services of a good attorney are expensive. Except for special services, such as incorporating your business (which can run to $1,000 or more), lawyers generally charge from $50 to $150 an hour and up. However, it doesn't necessarily follow that the higher the fee, the better the advice. It may be that the attorney who bills his or her services at $200 an hour is simply very good at collecting big fees.

Keeping Costs Down

Be sure you and your attorney have a clear understanding concerning fees before you hire. Don't accept promises of "fair and reasonable" treatment.

The best way to work with a lawyer in terms of fees is to ask for monthly (or other regular) billings and to understand what goes into those bills. Firms that are computerized will provide you with a detailed breakdown of time charges.

You can cut down on the hourly charges by being thoroughly informed on the matters you plan to discuss. For example: On that first counseling session to set up your business, do your homework in advance. If you go in with an understanding of the different types of business structures, your attorney won't have to spend an extra hour "educating" you. Make a list of the questions you want to ask before you meet with your attorney.

It's also reasonable to expect to invest some time and money in learning the legal intricacies of your business, especially at the beginning. You'll want an attorney who will teach you so that time spent in this manner will provide you with the skills and confidence to handle an array of matters down the line.

Your Accountant

Success means different things to different people. To some it means victory, to others, achievement. But to people in business, success is typically measured in profits—the reassuring black numerals on the bottom line of the financial report.

If you are among those who find the language of financial

reports—balance sheets and profit and loss statements—intimidating, you may be surprised at how your attitudes and motivations change when those figures represent your personal efforts. Not only is it a language that is surprisingly easy to master, but it's a vital and indispensable tool for achieving the success that's the goal of everyone who goes into business.

To state it simply: A financial report is a report on the health of the business. When the numbers are in good shape, a business is healthy. Only the numbers on a professionally prepared financial report—not a gut feeling—can tell you if a business enterprise is sound. If it's not sound, the numbers can even come up with the reasons, show where the cost leaks occur. Trying to run a business without an accountant is like going rafting in white water without knowing how to swim—dangerous!

How to Get the Best Accounting Advice

Don't look for an accountant in the yellow pages. The best way to find one is by following the same steps as in choosing your attorney. You will be spending even more time with your accountant, so this person must be someone with whom you are truly comfortable. You don't need an accountant from the Big 8—Price Waterhouse or Peat Marwick. As a small-business owner, you'd find their fees out of sight. And even if you could afford one, a big corporation accountant would be all wrong for you.

You need someone who's familiar with small business, someone who will take an interest in *your* business, give you sound professional advice, and keep you out of hassles with government tax agencies.

Don't be in a hurry to hire. Again, interview several candidates. Get a feel for their personalities, an exact estimate of fees, and a detailed explanation of what the fees cover.

A good measure of an accountant's skill and value to you is how he or she responds to questions. Some accountants like to deal with women clients; others can't stand it. That's because many women have two strikes against them—math anxiety and unfamiliarity with the specialized language of accounting.

Your accountant will:

1. Set up your accounting and bookkeeping systems and your system of financial control.
2. Organize your payroll system.
3. Prepare periodic financial statements.
4. Help you establish tax policies and prepare your income-tax returns.

In addition, your accountant may do a number of specialized jobs, such as:

1. Preparing loan applications.
2. Establishing inventory controls.
3. Doing cost analyses and profit and loss statements.
4. Setting up computerized systems for your business. (Depending on what you are planning to do, these may make good sense and are less costly and more timesaving than you can imagine.)

How to Cut Costs

You can go first class and use a CPA for all your work. CPAs are licensed by the state, must have an accounting degree plus two years' experience, and are required to pass a tough exam. You can expect to pay $25 to $90 an hour for this expertise. Should you opt to work with him or her on a monthly fee basis, $500 a month would be average.

Happily, there's a less costly alternative: to use a bookkeeping service for routine bookkeeping and let the CPA handle the more difficult jobs, such as setting up your records and controls and preparing reports, statements, and tax returns. Full-time bookkeeping services charge about $9 to $15 an hour, and you may even be able to find a free-lance bookkeeper who will moonlight for less.

If you and your employees keep accurate records of your daily transactions, a bookkeeper should be able to do your monthly entries in one day at a cost of between $50 and $100 a month. Or you may feel that it's more practical to have your entries done weekly. You can further reduce these costs by taking a tax-deductible bookkeeping course. Keeping records for a small business really doesn't present any major difficulties.

If your business is a single proprietorship, preparation of your tax returns will probably come to between $250 and $500. If you're set up as a partnership or corporation, it will cost half again as much because it involves two tax returns—your personal return and a separate one for your business. It's unwise to try to cut expenses on the preparation of tax returns. Mistakes can be costly.

Setting Prices

One of the most difficult decisions for a novice entrepreneur is what to charge for the product or service. Your accountant can show you how to arrive at your "break-even." This is done by adding up the fixed overhead—rent, utilities, insurance, consultants' fees, advertising and promotion, wages or salaries, interest on loans, projected taxes, and the like.

If, for example, your fixed overhead costs add up to $1,200 a month or $300 a week, your business would have to bring in slightly more than $50 a day just to break even. To show a profit, it would have to earn above and beyond the break-even figure. Nor is break-even the only consideration in setting a price on a product or service. You need to know what the competition is charging so that you don't price yourself out of the market.

It's harder to set a price on a service than on a product. A seasoned public-relations pro who went into her own business was psychologically unable to ask for the fees her abilities entitled her to. It was her accountant who finally convinced her to raise her fees. Later, she told him triumphantly that she had asked for and gotten $12,000 for a one-month project, and "the client didn't even bat an eyelash!"

There are times when a beginning entrepreneur goes the other route. This was the case with a woman who worked for a firm that supplied packets of assorted screws to lumberyards and hardware stores. When she was eased out of her job to make room for the owner's nephew, she decided to go into the same business. She knew the sources of supply, set up facilities in her garage, and hired two handicapped persons to package the screws. She had difficulty selling the product, however, which she priced at the same amount her former firm had charged. Her accountant convinced her she could undersell her competition and still make a profit because her break-even was much lower than theirs. Sure enough, as soon as she lowered her prices, sales took off.

A Few Words About Insurance

One of the fixed, immutable expenses of every business enterprise is insurance. The amount and types of coverage you need will vary with the kind of business and the number of employees you have. The main types of insurance you should look into are these:

> *Fire insurance,* which covers fire-caused damage to the premises, equipment, and inventory; *extended coverage* against such things as storms, smoke damage, and riot; *vandalism/malicious mischief insurance;* and *theft and liability insurance.* Many companies issue business insurance packages that include liability, basic fire, extended coverage, and vandalism insurance.

> *Liability insurance* to protect the firm from financial loss due to any claims of bodily injury or property damage in connection with business operations.

> *Crime coverage,* which provides reimbursement for losses due to robbery, burglary, employee dishonesty, or vandalism.

> *Worker's compensation insurance* to cover injuries and loss of pay related to employee accidents on the job.

> *Fidelity bonds,* placed on employees with access to cash receipts or other company funds, to guarantee against loss from embezzlement.

There are many other kinds of insurance, including business interruption insurance, key person insurance, and malpractice insurance for those in certain professional businesses. While all of them may not be applicable to your enterprise, some are mandatory. For example, if a bank or an individual has loaned money to your business, you will be expected to furnish evidence that the loan is adequately protected by insurance.

Health insurance, paid by employer or employee or both, is an attractive fringe benefit. It's available through trade or professional associations in many states if five persons participate.

Your accountant or your lawyer will be able to recommend a good insurance agent. Agents do not charge a fee. They get a percentage of the insurance premium. Therefore, it pays to ask the agent to do some comparison shopping for the best rates and to show you the results of his or her labors.

CHAPTER 5

Charting Your Course

Tips for Basic Record Keeping

any new entrepreneurs shy away from accounting and record keeping because they find these activities tedious or believe they can't cope with figures. But every business that is to succeed has a need for the orderly collection and recording of quantitative (numerical) information.

This information will fulfill two major needs. First, you will use it in order to run your company. You might think of this as an internal use. For example, your records tell you if your cost of sales is too high. According to savvy retailers, cost of sales—wholesale merchandise price, labor, overhead, and promotional expenses—should typically be 50 to 52 percent of what you charge for a product. If your cost of sales is 65 percent, that's a red flag that tells you to cut back on those costs—or else!

Your records can also tell you if salaries or wages are exceeding a profitable percentage of sales, roughly between 12 and 20 percent. More than 20 percent is another red flag, a warning that your enterprise has a dangerous cost leak that could sink you.

This information also has external uses—specifically, it permits you to report the results of your labor to the outside world.

Your records will tell the government everything it needs to know, information you are by law obliged to give. They provide the data used by your bank and your creditors to determine whether you're a good credit risk.

Thereby hangs a mournful but instructive tale. Several years ago a talented young designer received a $500,000 order from a specialty shop with branches across the country. To fill the order he needed to borrow money for fabric and for additional employees, but in his eight years in business he had kept only the sketchiest of records.

He lost that account, but today his records are kept in apple-pie order. He knows now that a bank won't lend money on the basis of a big order; orders can be canceled. Loans are made on the borrower's ability to show proof of profitability.

The internal and external purposes of your business's financial history, while drawn from the same data base, are really quite different. In the first instance, you will use this information to look ahead. It will show you where you are going and what problems need attention. The second function is primarily historical—a record of what you have already accomplished.

If you plan to operate within the business community—any American business community—the form in which you keep this information is almost as important as its substance. The IRS and potential creditors and investors will expect you to follow what are commonly called *standard accounting procedures*.

The Language of Accounting

Accounting, as well as its offspring, bookkeeping, is both a language and a function. It's a means of communication, complete with its own vocabulary, throughout the entire business community. You would do well to master at least the rudiments of this language, since it is risky to depend totally on others to handle this aspect of your business. Your accountant and book-keeper can provide some initial assistance, and you can read books on the subject or attend classes at a local community college or university extension division. Once you have mas-

tered basic accounting procedures and can speak about such
matters authoritatively, you will be taken more seriously by
those you wish to borrow money from or do business with.
This is because there is often an unspoken bias that those who
are savvy about accounting are better business risks.

Record Keeping: The Simpler, The Better

While it is advisable to become personally sophisticated, your
bookkeeping system should be simple, not complicated. It
should be easy to handle and understand, accurate, and consistent. Most important, it should tell you everything you need to
know about your business. It should include:

1. A daily summary of cash receipts taken from sales receipts, register tapes, or charge slips. (In a service business you would keep a record of expenses, labor, and
   time charges with a fixed additional percentage for overhead.)
2. An expense ledger on which you tally both cash and
   checks disbursed for expenses such as rent, payroll, and
   accounts payable (what you owe).
3. An inventory purchase journal showing shipments received, accounts payable, and cash available for future
   purchases.
4. An employee compensation record listing hours, pay,
   and deductions withheld for both part-time and full-
   time workers.
5. A record of accounts receivable (what is owed you) for
   credit sales.

From these records, three products vital to the functioning
of your business are generated:

1. Inventory control information
2. Information for your profit and loss statement
3. Information for your tax payments

Inventory control systems run the gamut from a casual checking of the shelves to complicated computer runs. Keeping track of inventory lets you know when to order, how much to order, how much each product costs, and how long a supply may last. In some cases inventory should be taken daily. Inventory control systems are often available through your suppliers and from some banks.

The profit and loss statement reflects sales and expenses. During your first year in business, it's wise to prepare a monthly profit and loss statement. This cannot be done without accurate records.

Today's entrepreneur must also operate within the guidelines and legal parameters of local, county, state, and federal agencies. All require accurate business records.

If you engage in selling goods, you must file sales-tax reports. If you open a business under any name other than your own—Circe's Temptations and Lotus Eaters are examples—you are required to file a Fictitious Name Statement and pay a filing fee to the county, usually at the county clerk's office. If you employ help, there are various taxes that must be withheld from salaries and matched by you, the employer. These withholding taxes must be deposited at stated times and budgeted in advance. Inventory taxes are based on the actual dollar amount of inventory you have at a specific date and are payable at a specific time.

To say nothing of income taxes—city, state, and federal. These must all be budgeted in advance.

Your accountant and attorney will advise you as to which taxes are applicable to your business. Be sure to include tax payments coming due in your annual projections so you're not caught short when the time comes. A master calendar on which you note dates and amounts of taxes, interest on loans, insurance premiums, and the like can be very useful.

Bookkeeping Is Like Housekeeping

A good housekeeper likes to have an orderly home with a place for everything and everything in its place. That's the function of bookkeeping in business.

Make it a habit to record transactions the day they happen. Do it while the transaction is still fresh in your mind and the receipts are at hand. Your books should account for every penny coming in and going out of your business.

If you have a strong entrepreneurial drive and give birth to a new idea every minute but hate detail, you'd better hire someone to take care of the nitty-gritty, because without accurate records the odds are against your business surviving. Most beginning businesses fail because of poor management, and accurate records are the foundation of good management.

You have a choice of two bookkeeping systems: *single entry* or *double entry*. The single entry system is a simple record of money going out and coming in. You keep a record of every dollar earned—the date, the amount, and a description of the transaction. But if you have outstanding accounts receivable at the end of the month (money owed to you by customers who have bought on credit), the single entry system doesn't give the entire picture.

It's good business practice . . .

1. To keep your personal cash separate from cash generated by your business.
2. To use a business bank account—separate from your personal account—and to make deposits daily.
3. To record all incoming cash—the amount, the source, the date.
4. To pay all business bills by check.
5. To get a signed receipt for occasional cash payments from petty cash.
6. To make disbursements (payments) from your business bank account only when you've received an invoice.
7. To keep receipts of all business expenses.

Your part-time or full-time bookkeeper is essential to the smooth and successful functioning of your business. It's a good idea to ask your accountant to screen anybody you contemplate hiring. The accountant will want someone familiar with the system he or she has set up. What's more, accountants have standard tests (like typing tests for secretaries) that are good screening devices.

The Good News

As a small-business owner you are entitled to some very attractive tax benefits, but there *must* be records to support your deductions. All legitimate expenses incurred in the course of operating a business are deductible. If you use your car or your home for business purposes, mileage, gas, and so forth are deductible and the room or rooms you use in your home can be prorated for tax purposes.

Entertaining clients is deductible. So is attending a business convention. If your husband is listed as a part owner or partner, he can go along, and his expenses will also be tax deductible. Caution: Stay within the bounds of probability. If you go overboard on entertaining expenses, you can be sure the IRS will call you in. Moderation plus accurate records to support your deductions are the keys to tax advantages that stick.

Success in business is built on an infinite capacity for taking pains. As a small-business owner you stand—or fall—on your records.

CHAPTER 6

Money Demystified

A Capital Subject

inancing a business is one of the major hurdles you have to face and surmount. Without adequate funding to launch and keep it going until it shows a profit, a business has little chance of surviving.

The amount of money required to start a business varies according to the kind of business it is, start-up costs, inventory, rent, and other expenses. In estimating financial requirements, remember that a business requires two kinds of funds.

The first is *working capital* or working cash. This is money for buying and replenishing inventory, paying salaries (including your own), and the day-to-day and month-to-month expenses like rent, utilities, insurance, and taxes.

The second is money for *capital expenditures* such as major equipment and improvements on the place of business. This money also pays for start-up costs, including decorating, telephone installation, display announcements, and advertising.

As the prospective owner of a new business, one of your first priorities should be to sit down with pencil and paper and carefully project what the above requirements will entail in terms of money. This is known as doing a feasibility study. Budgets or financial projections—forecasts of expenses and income—are part of this study and should be made every month during the first few years.

This is by no means a theoretical exercise. Your financial projections will form the basis on which your application for a loan will be made. Any potential lender will scrutinize your projections very carefully, for they'll show how much you know about your prospective business.

You will need an accountant's help in preparing your projections. Once developed, these projections become a business tool that you'll use constantly to measure the actual progress of your enterprise against your forecasts.

Your projections should show:

1. *Anticipated sales volume by month.* If you're going to carry several categories of products, such as clothing, gifts, and cosmetics, itemize your sales projection for each category. If your business is seasonal (stores that specialize in gardening tools, ski accessories, or barbecue equipment are examples of seasonal businesses), project the predictable ups and downs of sales. In a service business you would project the number of clients customers and multiply by your charges to arrive at an anticipated monthly gross.

2. *Estimated expenses per month.* This will include salaries, rent, advertising, utilities, office supplies, postage, telephone, and insurance. Some of your expenses, such as accounting or legal fees, insurance premiums, and various taxes, may occur quarterly.

3. Any *expenses unique to your business* or location, such as fees you may have to pay as a tenant in a shopping center or mall.

4. *Start-up costs,* including purchase of equipment, initial inventories and supplies, decorating, deposits for taxes and utilities, telephone installation, and the like.

When you've completed these projections and added 12 percent as a hedge against inflation, you will know how much money you need. Now, the next step is to go out and get the money. But be forewarned: any potential lender will want facts, plenty of facts, all the facts you can muster. It's not enough for those facts to be down in black and white. They must also be indelibly engraved on your brain. When you approach somebody for a loan, you must be able to present them forcefully, convincingly, persuasively.

When you apply for a loan you are, literally, selling yourself—your expertise, your business know-how, your ability, your brains. Making a loan presentation may be the most important selling job you will ever do in your life!

A projection of anticipated expenses is only part of a financial proposal. You will be expected to define in a written narrative form what your business will do, why there is a need for it, who the competition is, how well they are doing, and how and why your proposed enterprise can compete successfully.

These topics should be covered in depth. Spell out how you plan to proceed and how much money you estimate you will make. Analyze your potential market, describe your marketing plan, and list the methods you plan to use to attract customers away from the competition. Financial projections for at least the first year—preferably for two or three—should be included.

A potential lender will also want to know about *you*—what your business background is. He or she will expect financial and personal references and will want to see a statement of your current worth, including savings, investments, and outstanding debts.

With these vital statistics in writing, you are ready to approach possible sources of funding. Remember that potential lenders expect you to put more than your talent on the line. They want to see your own savings invested in your idea, on the theory that the more your risk, the harder you'll work to make your business a success. If you're able to raise 50 percent, or close to it, of the seed money from direct sources—yourself, your family and friends—you have a better chance of getting a loan.

The loan will have to be secured by collateral—your house, real estate, stocks and bonds—and be guaranteed by you, your spouse, or a financially responsible friend or relative.

Sources of Funding

With current interest rates peaking to 20 percent and more, a small-business entrepreneur would be well advised to look for initial financing or seed money among friends, relatives, and possible partners. Venture capital (in contrast to this seed money, which is often called adventure capital) is available to small businesses that already have a track record. Typically, venture capital is available only after an enterprise is launched and has demonstrated its potential for growth. The company or individual who invests venture capital becomes a partner in the business, has a voice in management, and shares in the profits. The Small Business Administration has a list of venture capital firms, and your banker can also put you in touch with venture capitalists.

If and when interest rates return to lower levels, you may want to apply to your bank for a loan. The more prepared you are to answer a loan officer's questions, the more knowledge and expertise you demonstrate about your prospective business and your financial requirements, the more evidence you can show of your ability to run a business successfully and repay the loan, the more likely you are to get that loan.

Your banker or investor will want to know the following things:

1. How much money do you want to borrow and for how long?

Believe it or not, many people who come into a bank for a loan don't know how much money they need to borrow! Be thoroughly familiar with what your capital requirements will be and have an accurate projection of how long it will take your business to become self-sustaining and show a profit. You should also know how much money you will need for operating expenses—rent, taxes, insurance, utilities, personnel, advertising, contingencies.

2. What is the purpose of the loan? What are you going to use the money for?

3. Will the loan be used to purchase merchandise that can be sold before the loan comes due, or do you plan to use it for inventory, improvements or decorating of your premises, equipment, or technical help?

An inventory loan should be *short term,* the assumption being that selling the inventory will quickly produce the cash to repay the loan. A loan for improvement of premises, furnishings, and equipment should be *long term,* giving you sufficient time to repay the loan

4. What is your primary source of repayment? Will it be from the sale of inventory or services?

5. What is your secondary source of payment in the event that your business fails to generate the profits to repay the loan? Do you have any assets, such as a mortgage-free house, insurance that can be borrowed on, stocks or bonds, real estate? Because the market value for an art collection, jewelry, or stamps fluctuates, many bankers and investors consider them to be less viable as collateral.

6. Do you have the professional advice of an attorney and an accountant?

Bankers prefer to get a financial statement that has been professionally prepared. They also feel more optimistic about the soundness of your enterprise when you've consulted an attorney about the lease for your business premises and when they know that you've had legal advice and filed for all the necessary business licenses.

7. Do you have sufficient life- and business-insurance coverage?

When your banker asks about insurance, he or she is interested, not in your personal insurance coverage for such things as a home mortgage or a college education for your children, but in insurance coverage on your business. If your business is a partnership and one of the partners dies, the remaining partner or partners will need money to pay out the deceased partner's share. The banker wants to know if you're covered by insurance in case of loss or damage to fixed assets by fire, earthquake (in California), water, theft, or employee embezzlement. In many cases the banker may want you to take out life insurance to protect the loan in case anything should happen to you.

In addition, the banker will want to know if you have business liability coverage for damage to customers or workers on your premises, as well as product liability in case something you manufacture or sell causes injury.

8. How much do you know about the business you're going into?

This is a crucial question. You should be prepared to talk fully on the subject in terms of administration, marketing, advertising, and personnel. Previous experience in a similar business or specialized training and courses in your prospective field of business are factors that will favorably influence an evaluation of your loan request.

9. How much personal debt do you have?

The banker asks this because he or she needs to know if your personal debts will be a financial drain on your new business. The promptness with which you pay your personal debts will also be a clue as to how promptly you will repay your business debts.

10. What will your competition be?

You should know what your competition will be in terms of location, whether you will be able to offer your customers the same merchandise or service at lower prices or a better grade of merchandise or a better service at the same prices, and other detailed information that demonstrates your knowledgeability.

11. How much money will you put into the business yourself? Will you be the senior partner, or are you asking the bank to take on that role?

This is another key question. As stated before, the bank will feel that you are a better risk when the major investment is yours. The theory is that you will be more motivated to succeed to protect your own money

13. What do you plan to pay yourself?

Yes, the bank will want to know how much money you will draw out of the business for yourself. The bank will want to control the amount and would be happier if you didn't draw at all until the business shows a profit. This means you should plan to cut the fat from your personal budget until your business is on its feet.

All Is Not Lost If the Answer Is No

There are times when, for various reasons, a bank cannot grant a loan request. However, if the bank thinks your enterprise is a worthy one, it may recommend that you contact the Small Business Administration. If the SBA approves your loan, it will guarantee 90 percent of the amount of the loan to the bank.

There are two types of SBA loan programs. One is the *bank guarantee program,* in which a chartered bank lends you the money and the SBA guarantees 90 percent of the loan balance. The other, a *direct funding program,* is limited to those who cannot qualify under the bank guarantee program. Since bureaucrats move very slowly, you may have to wait six months or a year for a yes or no to your request.

There are additional sources of credit available to you. One is *trade credit,* a type of ongoing, short-term financing. Trade creditors understand your needs because they consistently deal with companies similar to yours. Trade associations and trade journals will acquaint you with possible sources. They may be willing to offer you terms to purchase your inventory. This could amount to as much as a 30 percent savings in the course of a year if you're also able to take advantage of discounts.

You may be able to finance your equipment through an equipment dealer on a contract. You could buy a $500 cash register with a $50 down payment and pay $17.25 per month over a period of thirty-six months. Or you may be able to lease equipment with an option to buy later.

About Interest Rates

Interest rates involve a number of factors, such as the cost of money to the bank, which may remain very high for the foreseeable future. The interest rate the bank will charge you also depends on your previous business experience and how you've handled your personal debt in the past. The maturity of the loan also affects the rate of interest. Generally, the shorter the loan, the lower the interest rate; the longer the loan period, the higher the interest rate, because there's more risk involved in a longer loan.

The collateral you offer also affects the interest rate. If you offer your term savings account as collateral, you'll be charged a lower rate of interest than if your collateral consists of accounts receivable.

Level with your loan officer. If he or she discovers you are not telling the truth about some insignificant detail, your credibility will be damaged. And don't make promises you can't keep. If you ask for a loan of $20,000 and the banker is willing to let you have it for 60 days but you know you're not going to be able to pay it back for at least 90 days, say so. Don't accept a loan on terms that are unrealistic and unattainable. If you want to receive further loans, you must honor your debt obligations punctually.

Establish Credit-Ability

Even if you're going to operate as a free-lance business, open a business checking account. It's both professional and practical to keep business accounts separate from personal ones, even if they're both at the same bank.

Establishing credit is a must. A single working woman begins to establish credit when she opens a bank account, takes a personal loan, or acquires credit cards. It's wise for a married woman to establish her own financial identity apart from her husband's. She should have credit cards in her own name and her own personal checking account.

A good way to establish financial responsibility is to take out a small loan—say, for a car or home improvement—and pay it back promptly. Even if you're richer than a Rockefeller, make it a point to establish a sound credit rating. Credit is simply a supplier's or lender's belief that you will pay your bills. The more punctually you meet your financial obligations, the more credit-ability you will have.

Your Bank and Your Banker

Before you settle on a bank, do a little research. Sometimes a small business gets lost in the shuffle in a very big bank. Look into the possibility of a smaller bank.

Become acquainted with the loan officer before you approach him or her for a loan. The best way to meet your banker is through an introduction from a reputable business person, an attorney, or accountant. Failing that, introduce yourself. Say you plan to go into business soon. Invite the officer to lunch.

Try to establish a rapport with your banker. He or she will have access to information you need, will know how to tailor your request to the bank, and will be able to suggest which of the multitude of banking services available are relevant to your needs.

Do Your Homework

If you're serious about going into business, do your homework thoroughly. Devote the time and effort it will take to complete an accurate and meaningful business plan. Doing this will teach you a great deal about your prospective enterprise. You will find out what the chances for success really are. You'll have a more specific sense of how much money you will require.

The sample business plan for La Boutique that follows is meant to be used as a guide. Your business will be different, your input will be different, your money needs and experience will be different. But it should give you an idea of the solid information that you must include in your business plan in order to convince a potential lender that you have what it takes to run a successful venture.

Knowing and preparing for your monetary needs will not guarantee success, but starting with a firm financial foundation *will* give you a foot up the ladder and make it possible for you to climb to the top.

CHAPTER 7

A Proposal for "La Boutique"

A Sample Business Plan

U nless you have all your financing in place, you will have to prepare a detailed business plan in order to interest prospective investors. There are additional advantages in going through this planning process, since it forces you to think clearly about everything from expenses to marketing.

In this chapter, we have included a sample plan based on an actual business that received bank financing approximately two years ago. Only the names and location have been changed.

Most novice entrepreneurs prepare this document with the assistance of an accountant or somebody who has had previous experience in drafting business plans. The format is fairly standard, though your particular enterprise may require a section or two that we have not included.

A General Description

The sample business plan and financial proposal that follows is in two sections.★ The first section includes:

1. A brief statement of the purpose of the loan
2. A description of the business, including the market, competition, choice of location, competence and experience of management, personnel, and anticipated effect of the loan

The second section provides the financial data:

1. Projected profit and loss statement
2. Projected cash flow
3. Projected balance sheet

Your plan will be different from that of La Boutique, but the basic components—the statement of purpose and description of the business—will be the same. The second section, dealing with financial data, should be prepared or reviewed by your accountant.

It is also advisable to include a third section containing letters from former employers, associates, and business people attesting to the prospective business owner's expertise, ability, and financial responsibility.

★A thorough, well-prepared business plan automatically becomes a complete financing proposal that will meet the requirements of most lenders.

FINANCING PROPOSAL

La Boutique
234 Main Street, Chagrin Falls, Ohio 44022

To be submitted to:

First National Bank of Chagrin Falls
Samantha Wheeler
48 Partridge Drive
Cleveland, Ohio 44136

Purpose of the Loan

La Boutique is seeking a loan of $38,000 to purchase
equipment and inventory and to make the necessary
improvements in its newly leased shop at 234 Main Street,
Chagrin Falls, Ohio 44022. The loan will also be used to
maintain sufficient cash reserves and provide adequate
working capital to launch the new enterprise. The $38,000,
together with the $29,625 investment by the principal, will
be sufficient to finance the opening of the shop and carry it
through its first year so that this new business will be able to
fulfill its considerable potential and operate as an ongoing,
profitable enterprise.

Description of the Business

La Boutique, a fashion shop for women, plans to stock well-
styled clothing and accessories at moderate prices. The
emphasis will be on a wide variety of daytime and evening
separates that can be coordinated into go-everywhere
wardrobes. The shop will offer a personal shopping service
patterned after those of metropolitan boutiques.

There are 300 business firms in the immediate area of La
Boutique, employing an average of three women. Within
walking distance there are also several office buildings which
would give La Boutique a base of 1,000 potential customers.
Good public transportation should soon bring additional
business resulting from a projected advertising program.

Though in an older building, the shop, with the
improvements Ms. Wheeler plans, will make a handsome
setting for her fashions. There are six dressing rooms to take
care of rush lunch-hour business.

There is no competition in the immediate area. Stores
carrying comparable merchandise are eight miles away.

Ms. Wheeler plans to open the shop with a fashion show,
using well-known members of the community as models. She
plans to hire an additional employee to work part time, from
eleven to three o'clock, to handle lunch-hour business.

She will use vignette backgrounds for merchandise
display and plans to work with the local TV station on

fashion forecasts. Advertising will be targeted at the middle-income working woman and will stress the advantage of shopping where you work. Gross profits will range from 35 to 50 percent. On more unique items the markup will run from 50 to 60 percent.

Ms. Wheeler has had more than ten years' experience managing Polly's, a popular shop in Beachwood, very similar in type, price range, and fashion philosophy to La Boutique. Ms. Wheeler was responsible for the selection of merchandise and made four buying trips a year to New York. She also worked with Blair and Genesse, an advertising firm, on Polly's ads. She had personal contact with the fashion reporter of the local paper and was responsible for getting at least one or two fashion features on Polly's each year in the paper. She hired and supervised two salespersons. She recently completed a course in business management and bookkeeping at the state university.

Her customers depended on her to help them select their wardrobes; many of them plan to follow her to her new location.

Application and Expected Effect of Loan

The $38,000 will be used as follows:

Fixed Assets: automobile, store furnishings, etc.	$ 5,879
Leasehold Improvements	7,400
Inventory	40,000
Deposits	3,000
Working Capital	11,346
Total	67,625
Less owner's Capital Investment	29,625
TOTAL Loan Funds Requested	$38,000

The *fixed assets,* including an automobile for pickups, deliveries, and running errands, will be necessary to set up the new business.

Leasehold improvements of renovating plumbing and installing a new energy-saving heating and air-conditioning system are planned for this older yet excellent location.

Inventory takes advantage of volume purchases and discounts through established distributors.

Deposits for the new business cover rent, telephone, gas, electricity, and sales tax.

Reserve or working capital will be utilized for operating expenses to open the business.

Summary

La Boutique, a fashion shop featuring moderately priced clothing and accessories, will serve the middle-income working woman in an area with a potential of 1,000 customers and should soon attract customers from the vicinity. The shop will provide a specialized personal shopping service.

There is no competition in the immediate area. Ms. Wheeler's ten-year experience in managing a similar shop— where she was responsible for buying, display, and supervision of the sales force as well as working with advertising—and the fact that she has a loyal customer following are factors that should contribute to the success of the new enterprise.

The funds sought will enable her to purchase the large inventory her shop requires. Ms. Wheeler's successful completion of courses in business management and bookkeeping should further ensure the financial stability of her business.

She will repay the loan out of profits in equal monthly installments over a period of five years.

Explanation of Projected Profit and Loss Statement

Gross sales for each month and the year. Projections are based on analysis of owner's ten years' experience as manager of similar store.

Cost of sales. Projected at 75 percent of sales. This is based on data from the State Board of Equalization, Retail Sales Tax Division; The Robert Morris Associates Annual Statement Studies; Almanac of Business and Industrial

Financial Ratios; Bank of America Small Business Reporter and contact with the industry.

Gross profit. This is the difference between sales and cost of sales.

Controllable expenses. Controlled expenses are itemized below.

Salaries. This will be reduced nearly $20,000 by elimination of two clerks. The owner and family will operate the necessary hours with one employee.

Payroll taxes. This includes employer's share of 6.13 percent on Social Security; 3.8 percent on up to $6,000 of unemployment tax.

Alarm service. For use of burglar alarm service.

Advertising. For advertising in local newspaper, printing flyers.

Automobile. For expense of station wagon to be used 75 percent of the time for deliveries, pickups, etc.

Bad debts. For direct write-offs of uncollectible accounts. Based on historical experience of 0.1 percent.

Collection fees. Fees paid for collection of delinquent accounts. Based on historical experience of 0.1 percent.

Dues and subscriptions. For trade journals.

Boxes, shopping bags. For customer purchases.

Legal and accounting services. For outside accountant and legal assistance. Based on historical costs plus added service.

Office expenses. Includes stationery and miscellaneous office supplies like postage.

Professional services. For outside technical advice and assistance. Based on historical experience.

Maintenance and Repair. Projected on historical experience of 0.3 percent of sales.

Store supplies. For storeroom, cartons, etc.

Telephone. Projected on historical experience of 0.4 percent of sales.

Utilities. Electricity, gas, water, trash, etc. Projected on historical experience of 0.5 percent of sales.

Miscellaneous. For sundry items.

Total controllable expenses. Total of items from salaries through miscellaneous.

La Boutique
PROJECTED PROFIT AND LOSS STATEMENT

	Oct.	Nov.	Dec.	Jan.	Feb.	Mar.	Apr.	May	June	July	Aug.	Sept.	Total	%
Gross Sales	15,000	15,500	15,500	16,000	16,500	16,500	17,000	17,500	17,500	18,000	18,500	19,000	202,500	100
Less Cost of Sales	11,250	11,625	11,625	12,000	12,375	12,375	12,750	13,125	13,125	13,500	13,875	14,250	151,875	75
Gross Profit	3,750	3,875	3,875	4,000	4,125	4,125	4,250	4,375	4,375	4,500	4,625	4,750	50,625	25
Controllable Expenses														
Salaries	600	600	600	600	600	600	600	600	600	600	600	600	7,200	3.6
Payroll taxes	57	57	57	57	57	57	57	57	57	57	57	57	640	.3
Alarm service	30	30	30	30	30	30	30	30	31	31	31	31	640	.2
Advertising	35	35	35	35	35	35	35	35	35	35	35	35	420	.2
Automobile	90	93	93	96	99	99	102	105	105	108	111	114	1,215	.6
Bad debts	15	15	15	15	15	15	15	15	15	15	15	15	180	.1
Collection fees	15	15	15	15	15	15	15	15	15	15	15	15	180	.1
Dues and subscriptions	5	5	5	5	5	5	5	5	5	5	5	5	60	.0
Boxes, shopping bags	8	8	8	8	8	8	8	8	8	8	8	8	96	.0
Legal and accounting services	100	100	100	100	100	100	100	100	100	100	100	100	1,200	.6

													Total	%
Office expenses	10	10	10	10	10	10	10	10	10	10	10	10	120	.0
Professional fees	8	8	8	8	8	8	8	8	8	8	8	8	96	.0
Maintenance & repair	50	50	50	50	50	50	50	50	50	50	50	50	600	.3
Store supplies	25	25	25	25	25	25	25	25	25	25	25	25	300	.2
Telephone	46	46	46	46	46	46	46	46	46	46	46	46	552	.3
Utilities	90	90	90	90	90	90	90	90	90	90	90	90	1,080	.5
Miscellaneous	25	25	25	25	25	25	25	25	25	25	25	25	300	.2
Total Controllable	1,209	1,212	1,212	1,215	1,218	1,218	1,221	1,224	1,225	1,228	1,209	1,212	14,603	7.2
Fixed Expenses														
Depreciation	85	85	86	86	86	86	87	87	87	87	87	87	1,036	.5
Insurance	125	125	125	125	125	125	125	125	125	125	125	125	1,500	.7
Rent	300	300	300	300	300	300	300	300	300	300	300	300	3,600	1.8
Taxes and licenses	150	150	150	150	150	150	150	150	150	150	150	150	1,800	.8
Interest on loan	325	325	325	325	325	325	299	295	290	286	281	277	3,612	1.8
Total Fixed Expenses	985	980	977	973	969	964	961	957	952	948	943	939	11,548	5.7
TOTAL Expenses	2,194	2,192	2,189	2,188	2,187	2,182	2,182	2,181	2,177	2,176	2,152	2,151	26,151	12.9
Net Profit (Loss)	1,556	1,683	1,686	1,812	1,938	1,943	2,068	2,194	2,198	2,324	2,473	2,599	24,474	12.1

Fixed expenses. The detailed fixed expenses are itemized below.

Depreciation. Calculated by straight line depreciation method as follows:

Item	Cost	Life	Amount
Display cases	$1,170	10 years	$ 117
Desk, chair and file cabinet	578	6 years	116
Shelving	307	8 years	38
Furnishings and fixtures	374	5 years	75
1973 Chevrolet Station Wagon (personal)	4,600	5 years	920 x 75% = 690
TOTAL			$1,036

Insurance on inventory and building for fire and theft; also public liability, life insurance for loan and workers' compensation. Projected on historical experience of 0.7 percent of sales.

Rent. Based on new lease agreement at $300 per month.

Taxes and licenses. Property tax plus business license.

Interest on loan. Calculated on $38,000 loan requested, over five years at $10^1/_4$ percent.

Total fixed expenses. Sum of items from depreciation through interest on loan.

Total expenses. Sum of controllable expenses and fixed expenses.

Net profit or loss. Difference between gross profits and total expenses. Net earnings are expected to total over $24,000.

Explanation of Cash Flow Projection

Cash on hand and in banks. From personal financial statement.

Cash sales. Total sales less receivable due.

Sales tax collected. Estimated at 6.5 percent on 90 percent of cash sales.

Payments on accounts receivable. Collections from accounts receivable of previous month. Plan is to limit credit sales to no more than $1,500 a month.

Loan injection. This is the loan of $38,000 being requested.

Total cash available. The sum of items from cash on hand through loan injection.

Cash disbursement. Detailed below.

Owner's draw. Draw of $1,000 per month is sufficient for owner to cover living expenses, income taxes, and residential real-estate loan payments. However, this could be adjusted if the business so requires.

Cost of sales. Taken from the projected profit and loss statement, the second line, allowing thirty days' credit from suppliers.

Payroll and withholding taxes payable. Projected on the basis of one employee: 11.7 percent Social Security, state, and federal income taxes withheld; 3.6 percent on up to $4,200 for unemployment tax and disability tax withheld from employee.

Sales tax payable. Payments on sales tax collected for the previous month.

Setting up business, $60,000. This is the use of the $38,000 loan that is being requested. Owner is providing $22,000 to complete the setting-up expenses from accessible cash.

Total operating expenses. Total expenses including loan interest payments.

Loan payment principal. Only the principal portion of the loan payment is shown because the interest portion has already been included under fixed expenses. Payments are based on a five-year loan.

Total disbursements. The sum of items from owner's draw through loan payment principal.

Cash flow monthly. the difference between total cash available and total disbursements for each month represents a positive flow.

La Boutique
PROJECTED CASH FLOW

	Oct.	Nov.	Dec.	Jan.	Feb.	Mar.	Apr.	May	June	July	Aug.	Sept.	Total
Cash on Hand and in Banks (before purchase of business)	29,625											29,625	
Cash Sales	13,500	14,000	14,000	14,500	15,000	15,000	15,500	16,000	16,000	16,500	17,000	17,500	184,500
Sales Tax Collected	878	906	907	936	965	965	994	1,024	1,024	1,053	1,082	1,112	11,846
Payments on Account													
Loan Injection	0	1,500	1,500	1,500	1,500	1,500	1,500	1,500	1,500	1,500	1,500	1,500	16,500
Loan Injection	38,000											38,000	
TOTAL Cash Available	82,003	16,406	16,407	16,936	17,465	17,475	17,994	18,524	18,524	19,053	19,582	20,112	280,471
Cash Disbursement													
Owner's Draw	1,000	1,000	1,000	1,000	1,000	1,000	1,000	1,000	1,000	1,000	1,000	1,000	12,000
Payment on Inventory Purchases	0	11,250	11,625	11,625	12,000	12,375	12,375	12,750	13,125	13,125	13,125	13,500	13,875
Purchases						137,625							
Payroll and Withholding Taxes Payable (quarterly)			579		579		1,737						
Sales Tax Payable	0	878	906	907	936	965	965	994	1,024	1,024	1,053	1,082	10,734
Setting Up Business:	60,000											60,000	
Inventory	40,000						40,00						
Equip-	5,879											5,879	

													Total
ment, furnishings, and fixtures	6,121												6,121
Leasehold improvements	3,000												3,000
Deposits: utility, rent, etc.	5,000												5,000
Supplies	1,916	1,914	1,910	1,909	1,908	1,903	1,902	1,901	1,897	1,896	1,894	1,893	22,843
Total Operating Expenses Less Payroll Taxes Depreciation, and Bad Debt Write-off													
Loan Payment Principal	488	492	496	500	505	509	513	518	522	527	531	536	6,137
TOTAL Disbursements	63,404	15,534	15,937	16,520	16,349	16,752	17,334	17,163	17,568	18,151	17,978	18,386	251,076
Cash Flow Monthly	18,599	872	470	416	1,116	713	660	1,361	956	902	1,604	1,762	29,395
Cash Flow Cumulative	18,599	19,471	19,941	20,357	21,473	22,186	22,848	24,207	25,163	26,065	27,669	29,395	29,395

Cash flow cumulative. A $29,395 excess of current receipts over all current disbursements is expected for the twelve-month period. This indicates a substantial cushion for repayment of the loan.

La Boutique
Projected Balance Sheet

ASSETS
Current Assets

Cash on hand and in bank	$11,346
Accounts receivable	0
Inventory	40,000
Total current assets	51,346

Fixed Assets

1973 station wagon	3,450
Display cases	1,170
Desk, chair, and file cabinet	578
Shelving	307
Furnishings and fixtures	374
Leasehold improvement	7,400
Less allowance for depreciation	0
Net fixed assets	13,279

Other Assets

Deposits	3,000
Total other assets	
TOTAL Assets	$67,625

LIABILITIES
Current Liabilities

Accounts payable	$ 0
Federal income tax withheld	0
State income tax withheld	0
Federal Social Security tax payable	0
State disability tax payable	0
Sales tax payable	0
State unemployment tax payable	0
Principal payments due, long-term loan	6,137
Total current liabilities	6,137

Long-Term Loan	31,863
Total Liabilities	38,000
NET WORTH	29,625
Total liabilities plus net worth	67,625

CHAPTER 8

The Right Site

How to Sight It

T he location of your place of business is one of the most crucial decisions you'll have to make in your entire business life. Therefore, it is wise to forget your personal preferences and ignore what your friends say—unless they have successful businesses of their own.

There is some common sense involved in selecting a location. For example, a financial consultant will choose a downtown site where the action is. A copywriting service or graphicdesign studio needs to be near potential clients. A gym or dancestudio owner must decide where her clients will come from. Downtown is a good choice if your clientele is to be drawn largely from career men and women coming in at lunch time or after work. An afterschool play facility would do well in a location near a school or in a residential area where children live.

Business at Home

Many businesses can be successfully conducted at home. A number of thriving newsletters are prepared in a home office, picked up by a printer, and mailed by a mailing service. The two women in Camden, Maine, who built up Moth-Aways, using herbs with moth-repellent properties, started their business as a cottage industry. Another woman initiated college-campus tours that take groups of precollege students around college campuses; she runs her business from a home base. A successful hand-knit-sweater company was started in her home by a woman who farmed out the work to other women as orders began to pile up. Artists, free-lance writers, graphic designers, weavers, caterers, babysitters and shoppers, furniture refinishers (these need a basement or garage), decorators, and dressmakers can run businesses from their homes. Some eventually move into offices or shops, while others continue from their homes. Your accountant will counsel you to set aside a room or garage or basement that is used exclusively for your business. This provides tangible evidence for the IRS and gives you a legitimate tax deduction not only for the room but for a proportionate amount of lighting, heating, and telephone costs plus supplies, stationery, postage, and other expenses related to your business.

Choosing Retail Sites

Where to locate a retail business is a decision that should be made with complete objectivity. Resist the temptation to choose a location in your immediate environs unless it meets the guidelines discussed here. However, the high price of gasoline will deter you from a location that's too distant.

These are some of the questions you should ask yourself before you seriously consider any location:

1. Is it a good shopping area?
2. How many people shop there?
3. Is there adequate parking and/or public transportation?
4. Is there a shop (or service) nearby that's similar to the one you're planning to open?

Take your time. Don't grab a place just because a real-estate agent claims somebody else is panting for it. Investigate. Compare. Check and double check. Get professional opinions from your accountant and attorney.

Where, Oh Where, Should You Be?

When you're looking around for a location, keep these two requirements in mind: you must be *visible,* and you must be *accessible.*

The most charming little nook overlooking a flowered courtyard might as well be in Timbuktu if it isn't easily accessible. No dark corners or out-of-the-way cul-de-sacs for you, no matter how charming. Remember: A site's visibility and accessibility are directly related to sales.

Your type of business will be a major factor in your choice of location. If you depend on a busy lunch-hour trade, a place in the downtown business district will be your best bet, preferably on a corner where you get double visibility. A friendly little neighborhood bakery should be in a friendly little neighborhood, a college textbook store near a college. And obviously a toy store doesn't belong in a retirement village, or a ski shop in the Everglades.

Consider what kind of customers you hope to attract.

1. What are their shopping habits? Are you appealing to women who work in offices and shop at lunch time, to mothers of schoolchildren who are Saturday shoppers, to culture mavens who are evening browsers, or to well-heeled suburban shoppers?
2. What form of transportation would they use to reach your store?
3. What do the adjacent stores sell?
4. How long have they been in business at that location?
5. What is the quality of the neighborhood? Is it changing? For better or for worse?

Before you rent, get the store's occupancy history. If possible, try to locate the former tenant and ask why he or she left. Find out if any shops have failed there and why. Talk to the shopkeepers in the area and learn as much as you can about the neighborhood and the kind of people who shop there. You may even want to talk to the local police to get a feel for any problems in the area.

Basically you have two major options in selecting a site for your business. One is the strip shopping center, with specialty and service stores located along a main street and parking in front or in back of the stores. The second is the shopping center, a self-contained unit that is planned for a mix of tenants.

Suburban homeowners, the country's biggest spenders, gravitate to shopping centers where such attractions as art shows, bazaars, fashion shows, sportscar rallies, and antique car shows are designed to rev up shopping attendance. One of the reasons for selecting a shopping center as your locale is the interplay it offers with the other stores: the mix of shops provides a very high chance of attracting, sharing, and increasing customer traffic.

There are three basic types of shopping centers. The most familiar is the *neighborhood* variety, with 10 to 25 shops, where the prime tenant is usually a supermarket or drugstore or even a restaurant. The smallest of the shopping centers, it caters to the convenience needs of a small geographic area. The next in size is the *community* shopping center, with 20 to 40 shops, where the leading tenant is a variety or junior department store. Here you will find more specialty shops, wider price ranges, greater style assortments, and more impulse sales items. The largest is the *regional* shopping center or mall. It has from 50 to 100 shops or more, with at least one full-line department store as the prime tenant. When you find that a second or third department store is located in a center, you know it's a site that draws customers from the widest possible area. You will find, too, that the smaller tenants have been chosen to offer a wide range of goods and services.

Your Number One Consideration—Cost

Before you can consider any location, no matter how desirable, you must decide how much rent you can afford in terms of what you can reasonably expect to take in.

Business rental terms are generally offered on a square-foot basis. This can range from $2 to $100 a square foot, depending on the desirability of the location.

Be aware of the various interpretations given "finished" facilities. Try to steer clear of the "shell" specification, which only requires the developer to furnish you with four walls, a roof, and a dirt floor. You will have to pick up the tab for all the costly interior construction. A "half-shell" is a slightly better deal. It will give you gypsum wallboard, concrete floors, and maybe a toilet. What you should try to arrange for is a "key" specification, in which the developer supplies the tenant with complete facilities except for fixtures and decoration.

When evaluating rental cost, consider the condition of the space. If it's a turnkey situation, where you can literally turn the key, walk in, and set up business, your construction costs will be minimal.

In a shopping mall, developers extract the highest rent they can get. Although a full-line department store may be able to drive a bargain and get away with a rent of perhaps 2.5 percent of gross sales, small stores are generally saddled with a rent of 5 to 8 percent of their gross receipts.

In shopping centers you'll be expected to contribute to the maintenance of the center as well as to a merchants' association fund. If your shop closes at 6 P.M. and the drugstore in the center stays open until 10 P.M., you still have to contribute to the cost of lighting the center at night. Security patrol, holiday decorations, and central alarm systems are often hidden costs. Your attorney can help you ferret out the invisible costs that will become part of your rent.

Who Are Your Customers?

After costs, the next thing to consider in choosing a location is the kind and number of people it attracts. Do they represent your kind of customer? Find out by developing a customer profile, a prototype of the kind of person who is a potential customer for your product or service.

Will your customers be men or women—or both? Does

your product or service appeal to the young, middle-aged, middle class, blue collar, ultra chic? To mothers of small children, those with a casual or conventional life-style? To hobby-, sports-, gardening-, or fad-oriented persons?

It's only logical to locate where you'll find the largest numbers of your kind of customer. Talk to the other merchants in the neighborhood to find out what mix of customers they get. This will help you decide if it's the right place for you.

There are women who have ignored these guidelines because they didn't have the seed money to go into the neighborhoods they might have desired. Some were successful anyway because they had something unique to offer and were highly skilled at public relations. But none of them would say they did it the easy way.

Remember, you'll be judged by the company you keep. Take a good look at the other businesses in the neighborhood—will they complement or handicap your operation? If you're in a neighborhood of discount stores, it will be assumed that yours is a discount business too. If you're surrounded by chic, high-fashion boutiques, some of the glamour will rub off on you.

Estimate your space requirements. You will want the most space you can get for your money. Give careful consideration to the layout. It should be functional space with enough room to accommodate everything you'll need, whether it's desks and filing cabinets or display cases and dressing rooms.

Before you negotiate a lease, find out what the building and health codes are for your particular type of business. Talk to the building inspector and, if you plan to serve food, to the health inspector. You don't want to discover *after* you move in that you have to spend hundreds of dollars to bring the hygiene facilities up to code standards.

The best way to research a location is to spend a day observing it. Take a count of how many people shop there. See what the foot traffic pattern is, how many people come in and out of the stores nearby carrying packages. Talk to some of them to find out how often they shop, what they come for, and what they think of the area.

Try to foresee or anticipate problems. A woman who was starting a management consultant business rented an attractive office over a restaurant. It was a French restaurant that relied heavily on garlic as a seasoning. The odor, wafting up as she was meeting with clients, did not create the right kind of environment for her business. She had to break her lease—at a cost—and find other quarters. So watch out for pet shops, restaurants, and dry-cleaning establishments if you want an odor-free environment for your business.

If you plan to make additions or repairs, get your landlord's approval in writing and also have the place checked out by the appropriate authorities—building inspectors, the fire department, and the board of health—before you begin.

Negotiating the Lease

Read and have your attorney review your lease carefully before you sign it. Some of the things you should know are:

1. Who owns and pays for any changes made in the property?
2. How long does the lease run, and what are the provisions for renewing it? An option to renew becomes a critical part of your lease if your business is successful.
3. Are there any restrictions in the lease—or in the zone—that apply to your business?
4. What are the provisions for subletting or assigning the space?

The small print is important. Suppose you've taken space in a new shopping center. You meet the commitment and open on time, but the prime tenant doesn't. Will you be able to deduct a percentage of your rent until the prime tenant does open?

You'll have to live with that lease for a long time. Make sure it's a commitment that will work for, not against, you.

Finding a Quality Location

Moving is expensive. Look for a place that will fill your needs for a long while to come and choose a neighborhood that's on the way up, not down.

Locations will be enormously affected by energy, transportation, and environmental factors. It may be that public transportation will become a fact of life in the future. If such a situation arises, would customers have easy access to your shop via public transportation?

In the late sixties and early seventies, we thought the regional shopping center was the last word. Today, though, the energy crunch is changing that. As we go into the eighties, it's probable that shopping centers will consolidate into one-stop shopping areas with gas stations, cleaners, and food shops as well as boutiques clustered together in a single mall. Merchants' associations are already running buses into the one-stop shopping centers.

What about the water supply? If you are considering a location in an area where droughts could limit the water supply, make sure before you rent that your building has a contingency plan for obtaining water.

What about personnel? If you plan, whether immediately or in the future, to have employees, be sure there's an available pool of help within reasonable commuting distance as well as public transportation and adequate parking for employees.

Do your research in depth. Don't limit yourself to one source of information. Ask the same questions of several people and compare the answers. Whom should you ask? Other merchants in the area, the local chamber of commerce, the public information or public relations departments of the utilities (water, gas, electrical power) that service the area, real-estate developers, the city or county planning commission, and, last but not least, the shoppers themselves.

Consult your insurance agent to make sure you can get the insurance you need. Finally, your accountant and your attorney should be consulted before you make any hard-and-fast decision. Their experience and know-how will be invaluable to you. The rating sheet that follows will help you evaluate any location you may want to consider.

Location Rating Chart
Grade each factor "A" for excellent, "B" for good, "C" for fair, or "D" for poor.

Factor	Grade
1. Centrally located to reach target customers	
2. Availability of personnel	_____
3. Rates of pay in the area	_____
4. Availability of public transportation	_____
5. Parking facilities (customer and employee)	_____
6. Adequacy of utilities (sewer, water, power, gas)	_____
7. Local business climate	_____
8. Room for future expansion	_____
9. Taxes	_____
10. Quality of police and fire protection	_____
11. Cultural and community atmosphere	_____
12. Guesstimate of quality of location ten years from now	_____
13. Estimation of location in relation to competition	_____

CHAPTER 9

Help Wanted?

Selecting and Working with Employees

he day will come when your business has grown so much that you decide you need help. Or perhaps you will need one or several employees at the start.

Hiring an employee is an important move. It requires careful thought and planning. Before you hire anybody, remember that a retail or service business is only as good as the people in it. A competent, enthusiatic employee can be a Rock of Gibraltar and a major factor in helping your business grow. An incompentent one is worse than no help at all—and a costly mistake no business can afford.

Surveys have shown that a high percentage—would you believe 50 percent?—of hiring decisions are later regretted. They've also consistently shown that out of 100 customers who stop patronizing a retail store, 70 percent stop because of a lack of prompt, courteous attention. If you don't want to fire, be sure to do a thorough job of interviewing and checking references before you hire! You can find out how much and what kind of help you need by keeping a log of your activities for a four-week period on a chart marked off in half-hour increments for each day of the week.

Selling your merchandise or service is the visible tip of the iceberg. The other—hidden—administrative activities of running a business are time-consuming. You can find out exactly how much time they consume by keeping an activity flow chart. The chart will tell you when your peak hours of activity occur and help you schedule your time for maximum efficiency. In a retail shop, you should plan to use light traffic hours to renew your inventory, change your displays, do your telephoning, update your books, and so on. And when you're ready to hire an employee, the chart will tell you whether you need somebody full or part time.

Know What the Job Is

The trick in finding the right employee for a job is to know first what the job is. Before you make a move, figure out exactly what the job will entail, what skills are needed, what the duties will be. Take the time to analyze your needs. Then sit down and write an accurate and complete job description.

In a small business, you should look for employees whose skills complement your skills. If you're good at selling and hate paper work, you may want a part-time bookkeeper, somebody who'll take care of the inventory control, do the buying and ordering, and keep the books. If business management is your strong point, you may want to hire a full- or part-time salesperson.

Analyzing your needs beforehand gives you the best possible chance of choosing the right kind of employee, one with whom you may be able to form a lasting and profitable working relationship.

How Do You Find Her—or Him?

Once you've come to grips with exactly what you want in an employee, how do you go about finding this person? Start by spreading the word around among the members of your support group, your friends, and your business associates. Explain what kind of person you're looking for in terms of skills, experience, and personality. The word-of-mouth network often produces excellent results. One caution here: Many people have learned the hard way that hiring a friend is a mistake. If it doesn't work out, not only do you lose an employee, but you also risk losing a friend with whom you have been close.

Believe it or not, one of the best sources for finding help may be a customer. Ask several of your customers if they know of anyone—or if they'd be interested in joining your organization. This is always construed as a compliment and has never been known to offend anybody.

Other good sources for tracking down potential employees are school placement offices at both high schools and colleges. Employment agencies can help with recruitment, but remember that somebody—either you or the employee—has to pay for this service, which can be expensive.

If you wish to advertise in a newspaper, you might try running a blind box ad with a post office number rather than one with your name and address. This is a bit more expensive, but all responses will be in writing, and you'll be able to sift through them at your convenience.

If you can make do with a part-time employee, the local high school is an excellent recruitment source. In many cases students work part time as part of an accredited course in merchandising. They bring a lot of zest and enthusiasm to the job and can often fill a part-time slot admirably. And senior citizens on Social Security who can only earn a limited amount offer a good alternative. They may bring with them years of experience and loyalty to your enterprise.

Your recruitment methods will of course depend on your type of business, your location, and your personal preferences. The important thing is to find the right person with the necessary qualities and skills for the job.

The Interview

Have typed application forms ready to be filled out by each applicant before the interview. The short form that follows should provide you with the basic information you need.

1. Name:
2. Address:
3. Telephone Number:
4. Social Security Number:
5. Previous job experience (where employed, for how long, responsibilities, name of supervisor):
6. Educational background.
7. Other skills and interests that may be relevant to the job:
8. Character references:
9. Time limitations:
10. Any other questions relevant to your business.

The form should be filled out and reviewed before the interview. Keep it in front of you for reference. Interviews should be conducted in private in a relaxed, informal atmosphere. Ask each applicant the same basic questions; don't form an opinion in the first few minutes; conclude each interview pleasantly and explain, at least in general terms, when you expect to make a decision.

The experience of the applicant will often determine the approach you take in your questions. An applicant with considerable work experience will be easier to evaluate on the basis of past performances. With a less experienced applicant, your interview will need to be more in depth, and you may have to depend somewhat on intuitive conclusions. Look for personality, poise, ability to give direct answers. Watch out for tics or mannerisms that put you off. If there are any gaps in work experience, ask politely for explanations. When interviewing those returning to the job market, be sure to ask about volunteer experience.

During the interview you'll be able to assess many intangibles. Are the applicant's grooming and personality pleasing? Is the applicant direct and straightforward, friendly, outgoing? Does she or he seem confident or overaggressive? Ask questions that elicit more than a yes or no response. The objective of the interview is to find out about the applicant. To accomplish this, you must encourage the person to talk.

In hiring an employee you should insist on an image consistent with your type of business. You don't want a blue-jeans funky look if you're selling designer clothing or accessories. An overaggressive personality or a harsh, unpleasant voice are also to be avoided in an employee who will be dealing with the public. These are guaranteed to turn customers off.

Don't expect to find perfection. Look instead for motivation. Applicants you like may not have all of the skills you require, but if they seem intelligent, enthusiastic, and interested, you should be able to improve their skills with on-the-job training.

Explain to the applicant what the job entails, where it may logically lead in terms of promotion or opportunity, and what fringe benefits you offer. Make no promises you cannot deliver. It's better to be conservative in your description of the job than to glamorize it and end up with a disenchanted employee.

Don't rush an interview. The more time you take at the first meeting, the more you'll learn. Trust your instincts as well as your analytic reasoning abilities. You'll be working closely with employees, so it only makes sense to hire those with whom you are comfortable. Remember that hiring is a very important decision, so if you are unsure about an applicant, hold a second or third interview.

Checking References

It's amazing how many employers hire—often with unpleasant or disastrous results!—without going through the simple procedure of checking references. It is standard to ask anyone applying for a position to give three references, typically their former supervisors, who will have firsthand knowledge about the applicant's job performance. If you are seriously considering hiring an applicant, ask permission to contact the supervisors listed on the application form. Many who are employed at the time of the interview will request that you *not* contact their current boss, and it's fairly standard business practice to honor this request. If the applicant balks at your speaking to the others on the list, however, we suggest probing for the reasons.

Character references are especially useful if you are considering a student or someone returning to the job market after many years away. But remember that no matter how many nice things the character references say about an applicant, they may not know the person within a work context.

Most employers—even major corporations—check references on the telephone, though some may ask you to make your request in writing. Begin by explaining who you are and why you are seeking the information. Check the dates of employment to make sure they match those on the application form. Then ask the former supervisor to describe what the person's duties were and the quality of performance. What does he or she see as the person's strengths and limitations? Was the former employee the kind of person who requires a lot of supervision? Or is she or he a self-starter who is comfortable making decisions? What about honesty? Punctuality? Absenteeism? To some of these questions there are no right or wrong answers. They are simply meant to elicit information that you can then evaluate in terms of what you personally perceive as your needs.

Some former employers will speak very freely. With others, especially those who have reservations about providing a good reference, getting them to answer your questions is like pulling teeth. At the very least, describe the job for which you are considering the applicant and try to get a reading on whether the former boss believes this individual has the appropriate skills and personal qualities. If you hear something even vaguely negative, ask for specifics. It's also wise to take notes during these conversations and to hold the information you receive in the strictest confidence.

Again, you have to use your intuition and analytic abilities to determine the value of the information you are receiving. But if all three of the references you contact have reservations about the applicant, we suggest that you do likewise.

Legal Restrictions

There are some legalities to bear in mind while hiring. The Civil Rights Act of 1964 prohibits discrimination in employment practices because of race, religion, sex, or national origin. It is unlawful to ask personal questions about the applicant's marital status or family situation. In fact, all questions should be job related. Age discrimination with respect to individuals who are at least forty but less than seventy is also prohibited by law. (Apropos of this, you might remember that some of the most experienced and best employees fall into this age category.)

When You Find the Right Person

Once you've made your choice, carefully review the conditions of employment with the person you're hiring.
These will include:

1. Compensation
2. Hours
3. Benefits (vacation time; sick and personal leave; possible commissions; health insurance if available; etc.)
4. Parking

About Compensation

Check to see what the going rate is for the job you're filling. Find out what the other merchants in the area or what those in similar businesses pay their employees. And it's essential to give salespeople the incentive of a commission. Commissions are to employees what profits are to you. Commissions generally start with 2 percent of sales and advance to 3 percent as more sales volume is generated. Again, though, it's worth checking to see what the going rate is in your particular business. To be productive, a salesperson should generate six times as much in sales as what she or he costs in salary.

And Training

Once you hire an employee, it's up to you to train this person. Many potentially good employees don't work out because the employer has skimped on the training process. You have a responsibility to yourself and your new employee to do everything in your power to guarantee his or her success.

For the first few days (or weeks, depending on the situation), plan to take time away from your own work to spend with your new employee. Give on-the-job instruction concerning duties. Never be too busy to answer questions. Make allowances for the fact that many people are nervous in new job situations. It's essential for an employee to understand the job and how its responsibilities relate to the overall business. Remember, everyone has different working methods, so don't insist on having everything done exactly the way you do it.

While providing guidance, be sure to allow the employee freedom to do things in his or her way. You are the one in charge, but you will want to develop confidence and initiative in the people who work for you. It's the mark of a successful entrepreneur to be able to delegate. At the end of three months, then six months, and then at annual intervals, review each employee's progress. Be as specific as possible when describing your employee's strengths, contributions, and areas for improvement. Jointly, work out strategies to accomplish the improvement.

This is also a time to listen to the employee's ambitions and aspirations and to plan out ways to help the employee achieve his or her objectives.

Most people expect a raise at the end of the first year unless you arranged for an earlier review at the time of hiring. If your business is doing well and your employees are one of the secrets of your success, be generous. Loyal, competent, and productive workers are like gold and should be treated accordingly if you expect them to remain with you.

And Firing

It's also the mark of a successful entrepreneur to know when she's made a mistake. If within the first month or two you find the person you hired is not working out, either because of an inability to learn your business or because of some unforeseen personality difficulty, don't try to live with the problem. It's generally advisable to give some warning if you think there is a chance for improvement. If there isn't sufficient change, tell your new employee kindly but firmly that she or he is not working out and that you think it best to terminate the arrangement. Depending on the circumstances, you may want to give the employee an additional week's salary when he or she leaves. After three months of employment, people are generally given two weeks' notice or salary.

The growth and success of many a business have been the result of selecting employees who can assume responsibility and giving them the authority to carry out the duties assigned to them. An employee's ability to make decisions within a defined area increases his or her sense of responsibility and multiplies the employee's value to your business. Employees who reflect loyalty and enthusiasm in their dealings with customers and clients are an invaluable asset to the small business. These people are your representatives. Remember this when you hire.

CHAPTER 10

Letting the World Know

The Power of Advertising and Public Relations

Y ou're convinced that you have what it takes—a great idea, energy, resourcefulness, stamina, self-discipline, ambition, the will to succeed.

You've talked it over with your friends, your spouse, your children, your lawyer, your accountant, your banker.

You've researched the need for the product or service you plan to market. You've found the perfect location.

You've weighed the risks. You can swing the financing. You're ready to take the plunge.

Then the day finally dawns, and you open your door for business. Now you come to the heart of the matter: live bodies, known to the trade as customers or clients.

Where and how are you going to get them? The fact is that no matter how super your product, how unique your idea, how striking your shop's decor, customers do not materialize out of thin air. And it's customers—a continuing flow of people willing to pay cash for your product or service—who determine the survival and success of your enterprise.

Gone are the rosy days of the "Build a better mousetrap and the world will beat a path to your door" philosophy. Today competition is fierce, fast, and furious. The average person is bombarded with 1,500 advertising messages a week, all extolling the superior virtues of dog foods, refrigerators, reducing diets, presidential candidates, lipsticks, and headache cures.

To move merchandise off your shelves, you must attract customers—or you'll end up eating a lot of mousetraps. To generate sales (and that's the name of the game, isn't it?) you have to find ways to let your prospective customers know what you sell, what it can do for them, where you sell it, what makes it better or different from all the others, and why it's to their advantage to come to you to buy it.

In short, you have to advertise and publicize.

Oscar Wilde stated the case for advertising and public relations when he said, "There's only one thing worse than being talked about, and that's not being talked about." John D. Rockefeller said it in even fewer words: asked what makes people successful in business, he replied, "Others." How do you, a novice, go about transforming those others into cash-paying customers?

Advertising . . . Your Calling Card

Advertising is the calling card that introduces you to potential customers. The American Marketing Association defines it as "mass, paid communication whose purpose is to impart information, develop attitudes, and induce favorable action for the advertiser."

A good ad tells what the product or service can do for the customer, what is better or different about it, and why the reader, listener, or viewer should want it. But no matter how punchy and persuasive it is, you can't depend on a single or occasional ad to produce the continuous stream of customers you need to develop a successful business.

Advertising, like eating, has to be done regularly. Regardless of how small or large your business is, your advertising or promotional budget must be considered a fixed expense, like rent and utilities.

Take a Flyer

Let's start with one of the simpler advertising methods. Say you're opening A Cut Above, an independent fast-food restaurant. Your prospective customers are those who live or work in the immediate neighborhood. To reach them, your best bet might be to distribute handbills or flyers—single sheets printed with a pertinent promotional message—describing what you sell, its price, and the location of your shop.

You could hire a couple of dependable high-school kids to blanket the vicinity with your flyers, distribute them to every office, store, and home in the neighborhood, leave them under the wiper blades of parked cars, and hand them out to pedestrians and shoppers.

But suppose the product or service you want to sell—be it fashions, books, cosmetics, a travel service—needs to reach a larger market. For this you would turn to advertising in the media—newspapers, radio, or magazines. Television is omitted here because its cost makes it prohibitive for most small beginning businesses.

Who Is Your Customer?

Before you can select your most effective advertising medium, you have to identify your customer. Is your product or service something that will appeal to teenagers, college students, young marrieds, mature women, sportsmen? Is it for gardeners, travelers, gourmet cooks, grandparents? Will your typical customer be budget bound, busy, bored, leisurely, lovelorn?

Will your product make a woman prettier, save her time, energy, money? Is it an educational toy that will sharpen children's skills, a gadget that will make sewing easier or turn a brown thumb into a green one?

The product or service you sell determines the type of customer you need to attract. And that, in turn, determines your choice of media.

Before you read any further, sit down with pencil and paper and do a customer profile. Here are some questions to ask yourself:

1. What kinds of people will buy from me?
2. What are their annual incomes?
3. What will their average age be?
4. How far away from my place of business do they live?
5. What are their shopping habits?

The customer profiles for a corner deli, a record store, and a cleaning service will be completely different. The deli deals with neighborhood customers and should use fairly local media, such as the hand-distributed flyer described above, the local newspaper, the "shopper" transit ads, and window posters. A record store will reach its teenage audience most successfully through radio. A cleaning service, with a more widely scattered audience, will use newspapers, direct mail, and a listing in the yellow pages. *Your* advertising should appear where it will do you the most good.

Meditations on the Media

The daily newspaper has been the favorite advertising medium of retailers since colonial times. There are good reasons why it's still the small-business owner's best bet:

1. Because it is flexible—ads can be changed on relatively short notice.
2. Because it has longevity—readers can clip an ad and refer to it later.
3. Because it has the benefit of editorial assistance—food and houseware ads that appear on the same pages as cooking and home decorating get a helpful editorial boost.

Please turn to page 138. Chapter 10, Letting the World Know, continues at the second paragraph from the bottom on page 138 ("If there are several papers...") and runs through page 144.

CHAPTER 11

Yours for the Asking

A Personal Support Group

wo hundred years before Katharine Graham became publisher of the *Washington Post,* a woman printed the Declaration of Independence. Mary Goddard was the printer of the leading newspaper in Baltimore. It was on the presses of the *Maryland Journal* that she produced the first authorized version of the declaration, complete with the names of all the signers. She must have sensed that this was a momentous occasion, because instead of putting her initials at the end, she printed her name in full.

Some forty years earlier, Eliza Lucas, age seventeen, supervised three South Carolina plantations during her father's frequent absences. She set herself the goal of producing an export crop and succeeded in raising indigo plants from seed on the mainland for the first time. Thanks to Lucas, the West Indian monopoly on the dye was broken, and within a short time South Carolina was exporting 135,000 pounds of indigo yearly.

In 1880 a young New York woman was making $500 an hour as a consultant. Her name was Sarah Todd Astor, and her husband, John Jacob, paid her this handsome fee for her expertise in judging fur pelts.

The Women of Nantucket

Women entrepreneurs aren't new, although, it does take some digging in the hidden crannies of history to find them, largely because they're such a pitiful minority. As recently as 1971, only 42 women were listed as entrepreneurs among the 1,395 included in *Notable American Women,* published by Radcliffe College. Which makes it even more curious that in the late seventeenth and early eighteenth centuries, a small dot in the North Atlantic, Nantucket Island, produced a large number of women who were in business for themselves. A native of the island wrote that she could recall the names of more than 70 women who had "successfully engaged in commerce, brought up and educated their children and retired with a competency."

Examining this unusual statistic, Caroline Bird, author of *Enterprising Women,* concludes that for a period of time Nantucket was "a small self-contained laboratory with several of the conditions that favor the development of enterprising women." True, their men were away from home most of the year, and they were not burdened by continual pregnancies; also true that the island women outnumbered the men five to one and that funds for business were available from husbands' or fathers' whaling and trading voyages.

But there was an additional factor at work, a psychological one. Nantucket had been settled by Quakers, who believe in the equality of the sexes. The Society of Friends provided a climate of support, a network of encouraging sponsors for the women's business ventures. They served as what every woman going into business needs—a personal support group. A circle of friends, acquaintances, and relatives who will rally 'round with practical help, put their shoulders to the wheel or their hands to the paintbrush, pinch-hit as salespersons or stock clerks, act as tireless word-of-mouth boosters, find ingenious solutions to problems, and provide lifelines of courage, contacts, and cash.

Whom Do You Know?

The women of Nantucket knew the "right" people, those who would provide assistance, counsel, support, and a nurturing environment. We're assuming that most of you readers will have similar resources, people within your orbit who can become the nucleus of your own personal support group.

First, though, it might be worthwhile to examine some of our attitudes about reaching out for help. From the time we went to grade school and were urged not to look at our neighbor's paper, most of us came to accept the belief that what we achieved had to be accomplished alone. Boys faced similar training but had the advantage of participating in team sports, where they could experience the connection between cooperation and winning. Unfortunately, most of us had nothing similar to balance our early experiences.

Adele Scheele, the author of *Skills for Success,* points to another attitudinal problem. She describes a strange prejudice in our midst: the belief that there is something inherently wrong, almost un-American, about achieving success as a result of whom you know as well as of what you know. The absurdity of this notion becomes clear when we look at the life histories of successful people, which is exactly what Scheele did. They all capitalized on personal contacts and felt comfortable doing so. What we are suggesting in this chapter could be your first step in that direction.

Acquiring a Support Group

As the chapter title suggests, a personal support group is yours for the asking. Let's define it one more time. This group consists of a circle of your friends, relatives, and acquaintances. Even a stranger is appropriate if a friend has the perfect candidate. These people don't have to be your closest friends or the ones you see most frequently, but they should be people who have a specific area of expertise, something in their personal or professional background that gives them unique insights or skills. Include someone with a zany streak of imagination; search out people with contacts, especially money contacts if financing is your biggest problem.

Ideally your personal support group should be a mixed bag: both men and women, all different ages, a variety of professions, backgrounds, and interests. Five people is a minimum, and eight or nine are better—the more heads, the more ideas. They don't have to know each other. Part of the fun of being a participant in a personal support group is meeting new people, making new friends.

Don't be shy about inviting people you don't know well. Almost everybody is flattered to be asked for advice, and you'll find that even the busiest executive will make the time to spend an evening or a Sunday afternoon brainstorming in your living room. You provide the coffee or the wine and cheese—*and* the problem. The more clearly you state your needs and the more homework you do beforehand, the more efficiently the group can function and the more constructive the results will be.

It's an exciting, stimulating experience. When eight or ten people seriously get their teeth into a problem, they generate a lot of ideas, some far-out, some right on target. In fact, they're apt to generate so many that the air becomes charged with electricity and you can almost see people getting high on ideas. (Don't trust to memory—write everything down. You can do the weeding out later.)

Barbara Sher and Annie Gottlieb in their book *Wishcraft* describe the process in detail and call it "barnraising," a term that evokes images from an earlier time when people helped each other get a start. They suggest that these meetings occur with some regularity so that your support group can begin to feel a genuine investment in your success. They also advise putting some time aside at each meeting so every participant can have the benefit of the group's wisdom on a problem she or he is trying to solve. If you spend the last thirty or forty-five minutes this way, then everyone has found a forum for solutions.

How Does It Work?

Let's zero in on some real-life situations. Meet Ellen W., thirty-six years old, childless, and divorced. Ellen has been working as assistant personnel manager in an insurance company. Her immediate superior, head of the department, is only a few years her senior, and unless he's promoted or leaves, Ellen will be stuck in her niche for a very long time.

Thanks to the company's liberal education policy, she acquired a master's degree in psychology at night school. She also attended a number of career seminars and participated in group counseling. These activities prompted her to conduct a study concerning the company's method of screening new applicants for jobs. She rated it old-fashioned and counterproductive and gave her superior a long memo full of recommendations. She also devised an innovative set of questionnaires in which an applicant would block out five-year chunks of his or her life and answer specific questions about the goals, satisfactions, achievements, and failures of each period.

Her memo stated that she felt the approach she was suggesting would make screening of new job applicants far more effective than it was at present and also make it possible to promote from within on the basis of employees' strengths and abilities, rather than by the haphazard seniority method that was being used. Her recommendations and questionnaires were filed away in dead storage.

Ellen told the group that after canvassing the job field, she had come to the conclusion that she would have no control over her destiny, no chance to exercise her insights and use her knowledge, unless she struck out on her own. The seven people sitting around her coffee table were a professor of psychology who had been one of her teachers, a friend who was head bookkeeper in a factoring firm, another friend who had recently sold his first TV script, a graphic artist, the owner of a small fashion boutique, a homemaker and mother of twin three-year-olds who had developed a cottage industry selling sweaters she knit in her spare time, and a distant cousin who worked in a bank.

As Ellen explained to the group, she felt she was at an impasse. She wanted to leave her job and go into business as a career counselor, but she had very little capital. The apartment house she lived in had recently gone co-op, and her savings had been used toward a down payment.

How and where would she be able to get clients? How much money would she need to support herself in the interim? Should she work out of her home or rent an office? Where would she get the money to support herself until her business was self-supporting?

By the end of the three-hour session, Ellen's former college professor had invited her to lecture to two of his classes and use her questionnaires as the basis of a discussion on structuring job choices. The owner of the fashion boutique, who belonged to a club of suburban women, "every one of them itching to resume or start a career," had volunteered to set up a date for Ellen to come out and talk to them. (She did.)

The bookkeeper knew a therapist whose office, which he used only three mornings a week, was attached to a hospital. He was interested in sharing the space, and the cost would be far less than what Ellen would have to pay if renting on her own. Ellen took his name and telephone number. (The group had agreed that she would have more credibility as a professional if she didn't work out of her home.)

The scriptwriter had a friend who worked in an ad agency. She turned out to be a copywriter who was dissatisfied in her job and agreed to write a promotional brochure for Ellen in return for career counseling.

The cousin who worked in a bank advised Ellen to take out small, short-term, personal loans, repay them promptly, and take out larger ones, thus building up her credit rating. The cousin also advised Ellen not to draw on the pension-plan money she would receive in a lump sum when she quit her job but to put it into a Keogh plan, treasury bills, or CDs, where it would earn money and help her pay back any debts she might incur. Privately, later, the cousin volunteered to lend Ellen $10,000, which would be secured by the pension-fund money.

That's not all. Ellen picked up two clients after she talked to her friend's suburban club. She also arranged to conduct a group program with six of the members. Subsequently, the scriptwriter told a producer about Ellen. She was interviewed on a TV program and acquired two more clients. She sent her promotional brochure to high schools and community colleges in the area and was invited to counsel the seniors in one private school. In time, she acquired more clients by word of mouth and also made connections with personnel agencies to which she was able to refer some of her clients.

Small Wonder

Melanie P., forty-two, married, with two teenage daughters, had been working as a saleswoman in a fashion boutique for five years. She had a flair for fashion and superb skills in dealing with the public. Business boomed, and the shop's owner began to take her to New York on buying trips.

For the first few years she loved her job. Then she was bitten by the I-want-to-own-my-own-business bug. She wanted the satisfaction of being her own boss, making more money—and getting the tax benefits. What's more, she had an IDEA, an idea that could turn out to be sensational.

Melanie invited a group to brainstorm with her. It consisted of her husband, who ran a successful wholesale plumbing-supply business; the fashion editor of the city's leading paper; the headmistress of a posh private school for girls; a pediatrician; her own daughters; two bridge-playing friends who also had teenage daughters; and two friends of her husband, a bank vice-president and a contractor.

She presented her idea: to open a discount store of high-priced designer-name fashions for children aged five to twelve. She had done some research and found that there were no such shops in her community. The top local fashion stores carried a few designer at dresses $85 to $125 for young girls and had no difficulty selling them to affluent parents. But more significantly, at the local elementary and junior high schools, designer jeans and blouses and blazers, selling at astronomical prices, had become the standard uniform.

On one of her buying trips to New York, Melanie had visited half a dozen manufacturers of these clothes for young girls and learned they produced the items in limited quantities but would cut more on order. Her plan was to sell these plus a line of high-style accessories at a substantial discount, depending on quick turnover and quantity selling for her profit. There would be no charge accounts, no returns except for store credit.

The problems: the space she'd looked at in the prestige shopping mall in her area rented at $90 a square foot. Decorating, even using a contractor who was a friend, would cost a minimum of $50,000. Assuming she obtained credit from the clothing houses, she would still have to pay for merchandise within ten days of delivery to get the best terms. She would need at least two salespeople and would have to advertise heavily.

The group was enthusiastic about her project, especially the teens. The headmistress thought that twelve was the wrong cutoff age; fourteen or fifteen would give her the young teen market as additional potential customers. The banker asked her if she had estimated how much startup money would be required. Between $3,000 and $4,000 was her guesstimate. He suggested she sit down with an accountant and produce a detailed business plan with an accurate estimate of her money needs and a projection of how long it would take for the shop to show a profit.

When the group met again two months later, Melanie produced a watertight business plan: she would need $380,000, and the store would show a profit after the first six months. The banker pointed out that she was probably not a candidate for an SBA loan, nor could he recommend that his bank advance her any money, since she had no previous experience in running a business. He knew, however, of an aggressive group of investors with whom he could set up an appointment for her. If she could sell them on the idea and on herself, they might be interested in putting some money into it. As it turned out, they were—but only if she could come up with at least half the capital. Melanie's husband agreed to lend her $100,000 (borrowed against his security portfolio), and two brothers-in-law each loaned her $50,000. The investment group provided the remaining $180,000.

The opening of Small Wonder (the name was one of many the teenage contingent of her support group had come up with) was a benefit for a children's wing for the local hospital. Half of all sales on opening day were donated to the fund. The headmistress produced a celebrity hostess, a TV star whose daughter attended her school. The fashion editor devoted a full column to the opening and gave Small Wonder more space in subsequent columns. The shop became headquarters for preteens and teens and for gift-shopping parents and grandparents. And before the year was out, the investor group was talking to Melanie about opening Small Wonder discount shops in selected shopping malls in affluent suburbs near big cities.

But Suppose . . .

But suppose, you say, you can't come up with an influential support group. Suppose your husband can't provide a $100,000 and you don't know any bankers and your friends are men and women in middle- or lower-income jobs or homemakers having a hard time beating the inflation spiral.

Then meet Tanya M., a twenty-nine-year-old Russian woman who came to the United States with her sixty-three-year-old mother four years ago. They were allowed to come because Tanya's father, who had migrated to the United States many years before, was dying. After he died, Tanya and her mother decided to remain here. They had no money, knew scarcely anybody.

In time, they met some members some of the Russian émigré colony in New York. Through them, Tanya's mother, who had taught languages at a university in Moscow, got a job in a private school, and Tanya found a position in a bookshop. After four years of scrimping, they saved enough money to put a down payment on a luncheonette—but it went rapidly downhill! Tanya and her mother would have gone bankrupt but for the fact that in the evenings, after the luncheonette closed, they were running a small catering business. They had gotten started by volunteering to prepare the food for a party for a visiting Russian musician. It had been a splendid success, and a Russian ballerina who had attended the party had asked them to cater an affair she was planning. There they had met a florist who knew many of the "in" people in New York, and in turn had recommended them to some of his clients.

Ultimately, Tanya and her mother were able to get a loan to install a professional kitchen, and they closed the luncheonette and used the premises solely for their catering business. One of their clients called a friend at *New York* magazine, and in time a paragraph raving about the "Russian borscht, sturdy as a peasant," "the gossamer salmon mousse," and "the ineffable pâté— chicken and duck liver, cream and Courvoisier" appeared in the magazine's "Best Bets" column. They now have a staff of six and a station wagon to deliver party food.

Tanya's support group was picked up as she went along— but she had one!

Plain English, Please

So did Hilda S., who had graduated from Columbia with a degree in linguistics and was teaching English to foreigners in a New York State community college. Recognizing that the school's funds were in jeopardy and that her job was precarious, Hilda decided to jump the gun and go into her own business.

A friend who worked for a design and graphics firm and a teaching colleague were all the support group she had, but they were enough to get her on her way. The design-agency friend introduced her to the agency's president, who explained that copy was given to them by clients and the language was often fuzzy, needed to be sharpened. Hilda was hired to give a "Plain English, Please" course to the staff. The agency was so pleased that it printed a promotional brochure for her at cost. So far this has gone to some 200 companies and is beginning to bring in solid inquiries. And through the other member of her support group, she has a two-nights-a-week teaching job at the New School, which pays her rent.

Young Artists As an Investment

Leslie R., in her early fifties, graduated from college with a degree in art history. When her children grew up, she worked as a volunteer docent at the local museum, but after her husband died, she found she needed to augment her income. She invited a few of her friends to dinner one night and presented her problem. After some skillful questioning on their part, it became clear that her primary interest and area of expertise was contemporary art. One of her guests put her in touch with the vice-president in charge of public affairs of a local bank. He hired Leslie as a consultant to assemble and put on an art show.

Leslie visited a number of galleries and borrowed the work of relatively young and unknown artists. The theme of the exhibit was "Young Artists Are a Good Investment." It resulted in a number of sales and gave Leslie the idea for the gallery she now runs, which promotes young artists' work as an investment.

How to Reach Out for Help

In forming your support group, never underestimate the importance of your attorney, banker, accountant, and insurance adviser. Among them they have all the know-how and many of the contacts a would-be entrepreneur needs: they can give you advice concerning the availability of loans, the tax structure of your city, county, and state, businesses for sale, locations that may soon be available, possible partners.

In addition to your own circle of friends, there are associations and clubs, both national and local, that can supply you with contacts and information. The National Association of Business and Professional Women and the National Association of Business Women Owners can put you in touch with women in your locality. And almost every city of any size has a local group of executives and businesswomen who meet on a regular basis to exchange ideas and further contacts.

Women are—at long last—taking a leaf from the "old boys' " network that's existed ever since boys have been going to school. An "old boys' " network is a loose association of school chums and buddies in which the members go out of their way to help each other: the editor buys the writer's article; the congressman sees to it that his buddy gets the road-paving contract; the lawyer recommends a member of his college fraternity for a top corporate slot. Men have always been presumed to be more loyal, more willing to go out of their way to do a friend a favor than women were, but today women in networking groups all around the country are proving this isn't so. (See the listing of women's networks in Appendix B.) Women are counseling each other and providing a climate of support for those who want to move up, whether in the corporate structure or in their own businesses. We think you'll find, in fact, that there's help all around you.

All you have to do is ask.

Sandra Winston, a founder of Los Angeles Women in Business summed it up by saying, "A mark of power and strength is acknowledging what you don't know and whom to ask for help . . . Women's support networks have created an environment for asking."

If there are several papers in your area, how do you choose one? Say paper A has a daily circulation of 165,000 and paper B has a circulation of 98,000. Do you select the one with the largest circulation? Not necessarily.

You need to know more than circulation figures. You'll want a breakdown of the circulation of both A and B. You'll want the demographics (characteristics) of their readers—by age, income, sex, neighborhood, number of children, homeowner or renter status. These facts will tell you which newspaper gives you the most exposure—at a price you can afford—to *your* target customers.

While the weekly throwaway neighborhood paper, or "shopper," may not cover the entire community, it's a good bet if it blankets the area near your business. Ad rates in such publications are attractive, and people tend to read a neighborhood paper from cover to cover.

In planning newspaper ads, spend your budget on small ads that run frequently instead of on larger ads you can only afford to place occasionally. Have several ad variations and rotate them to keep your message fresh. You buy space in a newspaper by number of lines, and the more frequently you advertise, the lower the rates get. Be sure to keep a contingency fund of at least 5 percent of your ad budget for holidays and special events.

If you're selling fashion or cosmetics, you'll want your ads positioned in the women's section. If you sell pipes or men's clothing, an ad in the general news or sports section would reach a larger number of your potential customers.

Selling a nationally known franchised product is somewhat easier than selling a new product or service, since the personality and quality of the product have already been established. Ads for such products would thus stress the services and expertise your particular store can offer.

Most People Let Their Fingers Do the Walking

And don't forget the yellow pages of the telephone book. That's where people turn when they need a product or service in a hurry. Consider placing an ad in the yellow pages along with your regular business listing but only after a careful analysis of costs.

Airing Your Business

As an advertising medium, radio requires careful analysis. It's essential to know what markets a station reaches. If your business caters to senior citizens, you can't expect to reach them through a hard-rock station. Make a thorough study of the radio stations in your area and select the one that's targeted to reach your prospective customers.

The stations' sales representatives can give you the demographics of their audiences and will also have examples of what their stations have accomplished for other businesses in the area.

Radio time is sold in amounts of fifteen, thirty, and sixty seconds. Be sure the wording is bright and catchy enough to grab the listener within the first five or ten seconds. The cost of each spot varies according to the time of day and the size of the listening audience.

Public-access stations and cable TV in many cities offer advertising opportunities that should not be overlooked.

The Uncle Sam Route

While direct mail may be a potent advertising tool and can be targeted to any area or group of people, escalating postal costs make it expensive. Many people don't bother to open what they consider throwaway mail. On the other hand, a large proportion of hand-addressed direct mail with first-class postage *is* opened, and if the message inside is provocative and pertinent, your costs could be justified.

For mail-order operators, the choice of media is crucial. In general, daily newspapers are a less effective medium than the Sunday magazine and classified sections. Monthly, bimonthly, quarterly, and annual publications are used for mail-order advertising. You should choose the publication whose readers— homeowners, hobbyists, gardeners, sailors, collectors—will be logical customers for your merchandise. Advertising budgets of successful mail-order operators are often as high as 50 percent of income.

Be certain you make no misleading statements in your advertising. The Federal Trade Commission has set up rules that prohibit false advertising, misbranding, and any other form of deception.

Learn the Biz

In the United States a small business spends an average of 3.1 percent of gross sales for advertising. Retailers spend an average of 2.5 percent, while service-oriented businesses allocate 3.5 percent to advertising. Advertising costs for starting up a new business may run much higher.

There's no way you can become an instant advertising whiz, but you can learn a great deal by studying the ads in your local paper. Clip the ones you think are effective. Listen to radio spots and the people who deliver them. Analyze the components of a good selling message. Try your hand at writing a small ad for your business. A newspaper sales rep is an excellent sounding board and can give you valuable professional input. In terms of professional expertise, you'll do best finding and using a small ad agency in your area. A small agency can grow with you and you with it.

Almost every business capitalizes on Christmas. Many make an event of Mother's Day, Father's Day, back-to-school time, Thanksgiving, Halloween. Others put out the welcome mat for winter, spring, summer, and fall. And there are golden opportunities in trade category days. Try a Paint-up and Fix-up Week (for hardware stores); a Send a Flower Day or Decorate with Plants Week (for florists); a Take Your Family Out to Dinner Night (for restaurants).

One of the most successful boutiques in the Los Angeles area sends ten-dollar Christmas gift certificates to all regular customers. Since it stocks nothing under twenty dollars and has a 100 percent markup, the owner doesn't lose a cent. She says most people spend much more than twenty dollars, and the gift certificates create tremendous goodwill.

Tote bags printed with your shop's name and other types of distinctive and unusual wrapping are subtle and effective advertising tools. Well-designed business stationery and cards printed on high-quality paper serve the same purpose for other types of businesses.

There's Help Out There

The Newspaper Advertising Bureau publishes the *Newspaper Advertising Planbook,* an annual that contains a great deal of useful information, including graphs that show the amount of business done each month for a variety of businesses. You'll find these buying patterns to be a useful guide when you're planning your retail store's merchandising and advertising program.

There's other help available. Trade publications do stories about successful local campaigns that can be repeated in other areas. Manufacturers and wholesalers can often help you plan effective ads. They may even provide cuts and mats as well as suggest copy.

Some newspapers will put together ads on speculation for prospective customers. If you want to see what others in the same product category are doing, your newspaper rep may be able to come up with samples provided by the Newspaper Advertising Bureau.

Radio stations often tape a format or two for a prospective client. The Radio Advertising Bureau, an association to which many stations belong, furnishes cassettes of spots and scripts of commercials that have been used by companies in almost every product category.

Public Relations—The Brainy Way to Customer Exposure

Many people think advertising and public relations are the same thing. Actually, they're as different as apple pie and a chocolate souffle.

It pays to learn all you can about public relations. You pay for every inch of advertising space, but if you're creative and energetic, you can get space in a newspaper at no cost by convincing the editor you have a newsworthy story. You pay for every ten-second radio spot, but you might get five minutes on a news basis free of charge if you have an interesting story to tell.

Start off on the right publicity foot by making the opening of your business a newsworthy event. Some openings lend themselves to fund raising for a charity. A gift shop could contribute a percentage of the opening-day or first-week sales to a local charity. In any case, the opening of a business should be marked with a party.

A woman whose husband had the Latin American beat on a Washington paper opened a Latin American import boutique in a Virginia suburb. She invited the entire South American diplomatic corps, notified the newspapers, had a photographer on hand, and got fabulous publicity.

Saga of the Pet Rock

A prime example of savvy public relations is the story of Gary Dahl. In 1967 Dahl was a young man working in an ad agency. By 1969 he was a millionaire. It all came about because, after hearing people complain about the problems of taking care of their pets, he came up with a no-care pet—a rock!

To promote it he wrote an engaging little care manual that went to the owners of his four-dollar rock. If the rock seemed excited on first being introduced to a new home, Dahl advised placing it on some old newspaper. "The rock will know what the newspaper is for and will require no further instruction," explained the manual, which also told how to teach rocks to roll over—"hills make good training sites."

"Rocks are particularly good at sitting, lying and playing dead," wrote Dahl, "but shaking hands is out." However, rocks can be given attack training. In case of a mugging, Dahl suggested "reaching into your pocket or purse as though you were going to comply with the mugger's demand. Extract your pet rock. Shout the command, ATTACK. And bash the mugger's head in."

Dahl's Pet Rocks became a hot item, and orders from top department stores across the country came pouring in. He was soon shipping from 3,000 to 6,000 Pet Rocks a day. His ad budget was small, but every newspaper and magazine in the country gave Dahl's Pet Rock free space in the news columns.

Some enterprising New Yorkers even launched a newspaper devoted to Pet Rocks!

Some Ways and Means

There's a Merle Norman studio owner in Texas who regularly gets a spread in the news columns for women. She invites each girl in the high-school graduating class to her studio for a free makeup session and asks the local women's page editor to come by to interview and photograph the group.

Another studio owner devotes one day every month to beautifying the patients in the local hospital. She started when her mother was a patient there and discovered that the makeup had a therapeutic effect; when her mother looked better, she began to feel better. Now she does this on a regular basis, and the local paper has run several stories concerning her activities.

A caterer in Westchester showed how to make hors d'oeuvres on a TV show. A florist in Spokane demonstrated flower arranging to the local women's club; a newspaper reporter covered it, and the florist got a photograph and half a column in the local paper. A woman with a chic boutique in a Chicago suburb regularly provides the clothes for a semiannual fashion show given to benefit a charity—and gets covered by the press. A vet in Connecticut sent the local paper a news release saying he made house calls; the paper printed it, and he was swamped with business.

These people all learned how to advertise and publicize. So can you. Anything they can do, you can do—better?

CHAPTER 12

Climate of Success

Maintaining Your Family, Health, and Sanity

ore and more women are defining success in a broad, smorgasbord-like fashion, the ideal being to taste all the good things in life. Combining career and family, economic independence and a satisfying personal life are no longer seen as impossible or antagonistic aspirations.

What we've attempted in the previous chapters is to provide guidance about the professional aspects of starting and succeeding in business. But we'd be remiss if we didn't make some mention of the connection between the personal and the professional life of the entrepreneurial woman, recognizing that they complement each other.

This woman has her roots deep in antiquity. A famous example can be found in Solomon's description of the virtuous woman in the first chapter of Proverbs: "She seeketh wool and flax and worketh willingly with her hands. She is like the merchant's ships and bringeth food from afar. She riseth while it is yet night and giveth food to her household and a portion to her maidens. She considereth a field and buyeth it; with the fruit of her hands she planteth a vineyard. . . . She perceiveth that her merchandise is good; her candle goeth not out by night. She layeth her hand to the spindle and her hands hold the distaff. She maketh herself coverings of tapestry . . . she maketh fine linen and selleth it and delivereth girdles unto the merchant. She openeth her mouth in wisdom and in her tongue is the law of kindness . . . give her the fruit of her hands and let her own works praise her."

Trader, investor in land, manufacturer of salable merchandise, active and respected member of the community whose talents and energies found full expression, she could be a model for today's entrepreneurial woman.

Solomon didn't tell us what effect her wide-ranging, non-domestic activities had on her nearest and dearest. Did she find time before dinner for a quiet tête-à-tête in front of the fire with her husband, enjoy a little connubial dalliance in the moonlight under the olive trees? Did she sing nursery songs to lull her little ones to sleep, bind up bruised knees, go to sporting events with her older children, help them with their studies? We know her household ran smoothly; she had serving maidens.

Her Contemporary Counterparts

There is little question that the situation is more complex for her contemporary counterparts. Despite the emergence of professional child-care centers, fast-food restaurants, the microwave, and the shopping service, working women all over the land, let alone entrepreneurs, are exclaiming, "I need a wife!" The television commercial showing a woman whipping up an omelette, then a contract, and then in formal clothes, ready for a romantic evening on the town, may sell merchandise, but it doesn't bear a very realistic resemblance to the day-in, day-out lives of most women who are in the early stages of starting their own enterprises, when the hours are long and the profits are being plowed back into the business.

What's a Woman to do?

There's no set of answers on how to manage ("juggle" is a more accurate description) one's own business along with family responsibilities, a satisfying social life, and leisure time for rest and rejuvenation. Each woman's situation, problems, and needs are unique. Nonetheless, those women whose businesses and lives are thriving have created an environment that is personally and professionally nourishing—a climate for success.

We recently had a chance to eavesdrop while thirty such women discussed the subject and revealed some strategies they have developed to preserve and enhance their sanity, their families, and their health. We should note that most of the women in this group were presently or formerly married and most had children, a situation that mirrors the national norm.

Those who seem to have been most successful at avoiding family conflicts described involving their husbands and children in the actual enterprise. Nancy D. provides a case in point.

When her children reached their teens, Nancy, who had been an art history major in college, turned her garage into a shop where she sold the work of potter friends. In less than five years she ended up with a flourishing arts and crafts center in the outskirts of Cincinnati. Her attorney husband, fascinated with the potter's art, enrolled in a course and bought a kiln. Her teenage daughter, who plans to go into graphic design, taught herself calligraphy and hand lettered all the signs in Nancy's center as well as the invitations to openings. Her son won first prize in his high school's senior essay contest. His topic: "My Mother's Stable . . . of Artists."

The entire family vacationed together last summer, driving through Mexico to become acquainted with handicrafts south of the border. Next summer they're planning a trip through Sicily and the boot of Italy on the trail of lesser-known Italian crafts. "My business has brought us closer together as a family. Paul [her husband] finds turning out clay crocks and plates great occupational therapy, a relief from his demanding law practice.

My children are getting the kind of exposure to the arts they would never have found at school. I would say we have more real togetherness now than when I was a full-time homemaker."

"They Talk to Me Now"

Janet L., a former kindergarten teacher who opened a creative toy shop with another woman in a shopping mall, offered a similar story. She and her partner have a long day: the shop stays open until seven in the evenings to accommodate the working parents who are, according to Janet, her best customers for educational toys. Janet's husband is very much involved in her business—he does her books, built all the display shelves in the shop.

"Soon after we opened I wanted to attend a three-day seminar on how children learn but decided against it because it was on a weekend I'd promised to drive my son's teammates to a neighboring town for a hockey match and—the real reason—I was worried about how my family would react and how they would feed themselves. Thought I was indispensable! My husband made me go to the seminar, and my son found another mother to drive the boys. Bob barbecued hamburgers for the gang after the game, and my two children made breakfast every morning while I was gone. And they've gone on doing it so I can sleep a half hour longer and still get to the shop on time."

"What's more," she added with a gleam of mischief in her eyes, "they talk to me now. I'm a person, not just their mother."

Supermom

Trying to be a supermom to her eight- and ten-year-olds and attract clients to her newly opened promotional agency, divorcée Evelyn K. was heading, as she put it, for the loony bin. "I'd be up at the crack of dawn, cook the kids a nourishing breakfast, pack their lunches, deliver them to school. I'd arranged for them to be in an afterschool play group, and, happily, one of the other mothers lived in my building and brought them home.

"After a pressure-cooker day at the office, I'd rush home, fix dinner, wash the dishes, and do household chores until I was dead on my feet. I was ragged at the edges, becoming a full-time shrew. Then one night, when I was heading for the kitchen to do the dishes, I saw Jeff and David watching TV and thought, I'm doing something wrong. They're children, but they're able-bodied. So I plunked myself down on the sofa and said, 'Mom's tired. How would you like to do the dishes?'

"They do them now without being told—well, almost. I make breakfast, they fix their own lunches. And they're learning to cook. Hamburgers with exotic seasonings—nutmeg, cinnamon, garlic powder, you name it—they've tried them all. Weekends we go skating or see how many different kinds of birds we can spot in the park. Sometimes we throw a bash for their school buddies. *They* make the brownies and the lemonade. I'm not run ragged anymore, and my business picked up as soon as I stopped being so uptight. We've had some long talks, and my kids understand and are proud of the part they can play in my success."

The Home Team

Whatever the compatible and/or creative arrangements each makes, there's no doubt that a woman who runs a business that requires endless devotion and a major chunk of her time will have less for her family and friends. She won't always be there with the band-aids and cookies after school; she won't be able to drive her child to ballet lessons twice a week or pick up her husband's suit at the dry cleaners.

There's no doubt either that role changing makes heavy emotional demands both on the woman herself and on the other members of her family. If not perceptively handled, such role changes can cause major disruptions in the delicate fabric of interpersonal relationships. It's a smart woman who involves her family in her new career, makes sure they know they're an important part of her enterprise. She'll ask her husband and children—if they're old enough—to be part of her personal support group. In any case, children over the age of three or four can be part of the home team and take on some of the housekeeping responsibilities.

The members of your home support group may sometimes rebel about doing the dishes or making the beds. That's why it's so important for them to understand that your business is a joint venture, that they are your partners, and that *you need their help*. Everybody—even a child—needs to be needed.

Independence Is Catching

The women who had been sucessful at involving their families in their work lives—even if on the home front—felt that declaring a measure of independence from their children freed them emotionally. It provided an opportunity for the children to gain in responsibility and maturity. For the first time they were recognized and began to behave as fellow citizens of the family.

There was another fringe benefit. Because these women had enlarged their horizons, they became more interesting to both their husbands and their children. Their concerns expanded, their excitement and enthusiasm were infectious. Most families delighted in seeing mom in a whole new light.

The Family That Plays Together

Almost in unison the participants with families—husbands, children, or both— agreed that it was crucial to set aside time each week, not just to accomplish chores, but to share activities that the whole family enjoyed. In some cases these were business related, as in the case of the couple who spent their weekends in the country in search of wicker treasures. Many women described spending time in physical or athletic pursuits—jogging, bicycling, tennis, or golf—with their families. They were especially sold on this type of togetherness activity, with its fringe benefits of fitness and health. For others it was reading the Sunday paper and doing the crossword puzzle together or visiting relatives. It didn't matter what the activity was, as long as it was something they all enjoyed.

Sandy D., the owner and proprietor of a successful health-food store, described the importance of her Sundays with her family. "I'm divorced and have two teenage children. This time together helps me keep in contact and assuage my guilt. I don't like to admit it, but I'm still haunted by my years of conditioning which taught me that a mother should always be there for her children. I know it's absurd, especially since the kids and I are doing so well and I love my work. But if we didn't have our Sundays together I think I'd be in deep conflict."

She went on to reiterate a theme that was to be repeated in a number of stories. "I always use this family time to clear my head. It's easy to become obsessed, to think about nothing but my business. It's my nature to worry, and I don't believe this is a particularly healthy trait. After a day with my children I'm a new person, refreshed, alive in a whole other way, ready to face the week ahead."

In fact, some families held weekly meetings to iron out and coordinate schedules. One woman said her life and her family were in a shambles before she instituted this routine. "At work I was chairing a weekly staff meeting with obvious results, and one day it hit me that our family could benefit from a similar meeting. I discussed it with my husband, who loved the idea. He now chairs our gatherings, and everyone, including the housekeeper, submits agenda items."

Finding Time for Oneself

Perhaps no personal problem was more difficult for some of these women than that of finding time for the small pleasures that had sustained them before they began their own businesses. Sometimes it was friendships, lunches, or daily phone conversations with a sister or a special friend. For others it was trips to the gym or the hairdresser, tennis or bridge games. A number of women discovered they no longer had any time alone, time to think or read or do just plain nothing. One woman complained that she was seeing the world as an octopus, with its many tentacles coming after her.

This woman's entrepreneurial companions urged her to reassess her priorities. One put it bluntly—"Success isn't worth very much if you aren't enjoying it"—and described having suffered from similar feelings until she had arranged her schedule to accommodate her personal yearnings for both companionship and alone time. A number of others chimed in with their stories of neglecting their appearances or exercise needs or even proper eating habits until they had realized that if their lives had more balance, they would be happier, more relaxed, and better able to run their businesses smoothly and successfully.

These women all admitted that accomplishing this wasn't always easy but was certainly worth the effort. Some returned to activities they had dropped, and others found substitutes. If they no longer had much in common with old friends (which to a one they described as painful), they were able to make new friends through the trade associations and women's networks they had joined. One entrepreneur said she found salvation in the all-women weekend retreats in the mountains that her church ran. Another decided to get up an hour earlier three times a week in order to return to the gym. A third found a college student to live in and traded room and board for light housework, some chauffeuring, child care, and meal preparation. She used the extra time that became available to see old friends and have her hair and nails done professionally. With some chagrin, she reported finding enormous reserves of energy as soon as she no longer saw herself as a child deprived of cherished pastimes.

A Group Portrait

What emerges from these stories is a group portrait of winners, individuals who perceive themselves as neither victims nor superwomen. They have upped their odds for success by creating nurturing environments. They have enlisted the aid of families and friends, and when they could afford it, they hired help. They've also paid attention to their emotional needs and their physical health and appearance. They've accepted sensible trade-offs and have realized that it takes time to put all the pieces of a good life together, especially when one is making as substantial a change as beginning a new business.

Most of all, though, they exhibited a sense of humor and perspective about the very real problems, conflicts, and the other ordinary and extraordinary frustrations of entrepreneurial life. In essence, they had learned a valuable lesson: that the climate of success begins with the self and then radiates outward.

These women are among the hundreds of thousands of role models paving the way for others to emulate their endeavors. Whatever the risks they run, they are saying with their actions that the potential rewards are even greater. We include their stories here for inspiration and instruction. In a sense they and the others mentioned throughout this book are a mirror. If you can identify with their aspirations and personal qualities, you're on your way. We wish you success.

APPENDIX A

Small Business Administration Field Office Addresses

Alabama
908 S. 20th St.
Birmingham 25205

Alaska
1016 W. Sixth Ave., #200
Anchorage 99501

101 12th Ave.
Fairbanks 99701

Arizona
3030 N. Central Ave.
Phoenix 85012

Arkansas
611 Gaines St.
Little Rock 72201

California
1229 N St.
Fresno 93712

350 S. Figueroa St.
Los Angeles 90071

2800 Cottage Way
Sacramento 95825

880 Front St.
San Diego 92188

211 Main St.
San Francisco 94105

Colorado
721 19th St.
Denver 80202

Connecticut
One Financial Plaza
Hartford 06103

Delaware
844 King St.
Wilmington 19801

Florida
2222 Ponce de Leon
Coral Gables 33134

400 W. Bay St.
Jacksonville 32202

700 Twiggs St.
Tampa 33602

701 Clematis St.
W. Palm Beach 33402

Georgia
1720 Peachtree Rd. N.W.
Atlanta 30309

Guam
Pacific Daily News Bldg.
Agana 96910

Hawaii
300 Ala Moana
Honolulu 96850

Idaho
1005 Main St.
Boise 83701

Illinois
219 S. Dearborn St.
Chicago 60694

1 N. Old State Capitol Pl.
Springfield 62701

Indiana
575 N. Pennsylvania St.
Indianapolis 46204

Iowa
210 Walnut St.
Des Moines 50309

Kansas
110 E. Waterman St.
Wichita 67202

Kentucky
600 Federal Pl., Rm. 188
Louisville 40402

Louisiana
1001 Howard Ave.
New Orleans 70113

500 Fannin St.
Shreveport 71101

Maine
40 Western Ave., Rm. 512
Augusta 04330

Maryland
8600 La Salle Rd.
Towson 21204 (Baltimore)

Massachusetts
150 Causeway St.
Boston 02114

302 High St.
Holyoke 10150

Michigan
477 Michigan Ave.
Detroit 48226

540 W. Kaye Ave.
Marquette 49885

Minnesota
12 S. Sixth St.
Minneapolis 55402

Mississippi
111 Fred Haise Blvd.
Biloxi 39530

200 E. Pascagoula St.
Jackson 39201

Missouri
1150 Grand Ave.
Kansas City 64106

Mercantile Tower, Ste. 2500
St. Louis 63101

Montana
301 South Park
Helena 59601

Nebraska
Nineteenth & Farnam Sts.
Omaha 68102

Nevada
301 E. Stewart
Las Vegas 89101

50 S. Virginia St.
Reno 89505

New Hampshire
55 Pleasant St.
Concord 03301

New Jersey
1800 E. Davis St.
Camden 08104

970 Broad St., #1635
Newark 07102

New Mexico
5000 Marble Ave., N.E.
Albuquerque 87110

New York
3100 Twin Towers Bldg.
Albany 12210

111 W. Huron St.
Buffalo 14202

180 State St., #412
Elmira 14901

425 Broad Hollow Rd.
Melville 11746

26 Federal Plaza, #3100
New York 10007

100 State St.
Rochester 14014

100 S. Clinton, #1071
Syracuse 13260

North Carolina
230 S. Tryon St., #700
Charlotte 28202

215 S. Evans St.
Greenville 27834

North Dakota
657 2nd Ave., N., #218
Fargo 58102

Ohio
550 Main St., #5028
Cincinnati 45202

1240 E. 9th St., #317
Cleveland 44199

85 Marconi Blvd.
Columbus 43215

Oklahoma
200 N. W. 5th St.
Oklahoma City 73102

Oregon
1220 S. W. Third Ave.
Portland 97204

Pennsylvania
100 Chestnut St.
Harrisburg 17101

One Bala Cynwyd Plaza
Bala Cynwyd 19004 (Phila.)

1000 Liberty Ave.
Pittsburgh 15111

20 N. Pennsylvania Ave.
Wilkes-Barre 18702

Puerto Rico
Chardon & Bolivia Sts.
Hato Rey 00919

Rhode Island
57 Eddy St.
Providence 92903

South Carolina
1801 Assembly St.
Columbia 29201

South Dakota
515 9th St.
Rapid City 57701

8th & Main Ave.
Sioux Falls 57102

Tennessee
502 S. Gay St., #307
Knoxville 37902

167 N. Main St.
Memphis 38103

404 James Robertson Pkwy.,
#1012
Nashville 37219

Texas
3105 Leopard St.
Corpus Christi 78408

100 Commerce St.
Dallas 75242

4100 Rio Bravo, #300
El Paso 79902

222 E. Van Buren
Harlington 78550
(Lower Rio Grande Valley)

1 Allen Center, 500 Dallas St.
Houston 77002

1205 Texas Ave.
Lubbock 79401

100 S. Washington St., #G12
Marshall 75670

727 E. Durango, Rm. A-513
San Antonio 78206

Utah
125 S. State St., Rm. 2237
Salt Lake City 84138

Vermont
87 State St., P.O. Box 605
Montpelier 05602

Virgin Islands
Federal Office Bldg.
Veteran's Drive, St. Thomas
00801

Virginia
400 N. 8th St. #3015
Richmond 23240

Washington
915 Second Ave.
Seattle 98174

Courthouse Bldg., #651
Spokane 99120

Washington, D.C.
1030 5th St., N.W., #250
Washington, D.C. 20417

West Virginia
Charleston National Plaza
Suite 628
Charleston 25301

109 N. 3rd St.
Clarksburg

Wisconsin
500 S. Barstow St., #B9AA
Eau Claire 54701

122 W. Washington Ave.
Madison 53703

517 E. Wisconsin Ave.
Milwaukee 53202

Wyoming
100 E. B St., #4001
Casper 82601

APPENDIX B

Networks for Women in Business

All the Good Old Girls, Inc.
P.O. Box 20121
Minneapolis, MN 55450

American Women's Economic
Development Corp.
1270 Ave. of the Americas
New York, NY 10020

The Career Network
P.O. Box 3081
Everett, WA 98203

Detroit Network
c/o Phyllis Kozlowki, Atty.
1756 Penobscot Bldg.
Detroit, MI 48226

Executive Women's Network
Baltimore New Directions
12 E. 24th St.
Baltimore, MD 21218

The International Network of
Business & Professional
Women
11070 S.W. Allen Blvd.
Beaverton, OR 97005

International Organization of
Women Executives
1800 N. 78th Court
Elmwood Park, IL 60635

National Association of Female
Executives
485 5th Ave., Suite 401
New York, NY 10017

National Association of Women
Business Owners
2000 P St. NW, Suite 410
Washington, D.C. 20036

Network of Executive Women
c/o Lifeplan
40 E. Broad St.
Bethlehem, PA 18018

The Network of Women in
Business
9331 N. Washington Blvd.
Indianapolis, IN 46240

The Peninsula Professional
Women's Network
701 Welch Rd., Suite 1119
Palo Alto, CA 94303

Woman/Owner/Manager/
Administrator Networking
(WOMAN)
2520 N. Lincoln Ave., #60
Chicago, IL 60614

Women Entrepreneurs
P.O. Box 26738
San Francisco, CA 94126

Women in Business, Inc.
5000 Wilshire Blvd., Suite 1402
Los Angeles, CA 90036

Women in Business Network
Ralston Purina Co.
Checkerboard Square 6T
St. Louis, MO 63188

APPENDIX C

Sources and Resources

Nowadays there's plenty of help and information for the aspiring entrepreneur—books, booklets, seminars, courses, counseling, networking. Some of these sources and resources are listed below. You'll find many more in your local library.

BOOKS

Advertising and Publicity

Bloomenthal, Howard. *Promoting Your Cause*. New York: Funk & Wagnalls, 1971.

McCluny, Connie. *How to Advertise and Promote Your Small Business*. New York: John Wiley & Sons.

O'Brien, Richard. *Publicity and How to Get It*. New York: Harper & Row, 1977.

Smith, Cynthia S. *How to Get Big Results From a Small Advertising Budget*. New York: E. P. Dutton & Co., 1973.

After you master the art of writing a publicity release, you will need to know the names of the key editors to whom your releases should be sent. The best known are: *Bacon's Publicity Checker, Bacon's Newspaper Directory,* and *Working Press of the Nation.* You'll find them in your local public library.

Crafts

Clark, Leta W. *How to Make Money With Your Crafts*. New York: William Morrow & Co., 1973.

Genfan, Herb and Taetzsch, Lyn. *How to Start Your Own Craft Business*. New York: Watson-Guptill, 1974.

Financial

Gross, Harry. *Financing for Small and Medium-Sized Businesses*. New Jersey: Prentice-Hall, 1969.

Klimley, April. *Borrowing Basics for Women*. Free from the First National City Bank, Public Affairs Division, 399 Park Ave., New York, NY 10022.

Mancuso, Joseph R. *How to Start, Finance, and Manage Your Own Small Business*. New Jersey: Prentice-Hall, 1978.

Phillips, Michael. *The Seven Laws of Money*. New York: Random House, 1974.

Franchises

Bank of America. *Franchising*. A Bank of America Small Business Reporter publication. Send $1 to Bank of America, Department 3120, P.O. Box 37000, San Francisco, CA 94137.

Cameron, Jan. *The Franchise Handbook*. New York: Crown Publishers, 1970.

National Better Business Bureau. *Facts About Franchising*. New York: National Better Business Bureau, Inc.

Superintendent of Documents. *Franchise Index Profile*. (A small business booklet.) Washington, D.C.: U.S. Government Printing Office, 20402

A Business at Home

Bahan, Marian. *The Complete Book of How to Start and Run a Money-Making Business in Your Home*. New Jersey: Prentice-Hall.

Council of Better Business Bureaus. *Tips on Work at Home*. Council of Better Business Bureaus, 1150 17th Street, NW, Washington, D.C. 20036.

Hovey, Helen Stone. *Making Money in Your Own Kitchen: Over 1600 Products that Women Can Make*. New York: Wefred Funk.

Robertson, Laura. *How to Start a Money-Making Business at Home*. New York: Frederick Fell Publishers.

Weber, Judith and White, Carol. *Profits at Your Doorstep: A Complete Guide to Setting Up a Successful Business in Your Own Home*. New York: Barnes & Noble, 1978.

Mail Order

Simon, Julian L. *How to Start and Operate a Mail Order Business*. New York: McGraw-Hill, 1976.

Stern, Alfred. *How Mail Order Fortunes are Made: Everything You Need to Know about Mail Order*. New York: Porter, 1977.

General

Cahill, June. *Can a Smaller Store Succeed?* New York: Fairchild Publications.

Drake Publishers, Inc. *How to Buy and Sell a Small Business*. Drake Publishers, 381 Park Ave. South, New York, NY 10016.

Dun & Bradstreet Library. *Patterns for Success in Managing a Small Business*. New York: Dun & Bradstreet Library.

Greene, Gardiner G. *How to Start and Manage Your Own Business*. New York: McGraw-Hill, 1975.

Griffin, Barbara. *A Successful Business of Your Own*. Los Angeles: Sherbourne Press, 1974.

Hilton, Terri. *Small Business Ideas for Women and How to Get Started*. New York: Pilot Books, 1975.

Lasser, Jacob K. *How to Run a Small Business*. New York: McGraw-Hill, 1974.

Miller, Luree. *Late Bloom: New Lives for Women*. New York: Paddington Press, 1979.

Richert, G. *Retailing Principles and Practices*. New York: McGraw-Hill, 1968.

Scheele, Adele M. *Skills for Success: A Guide to the Top*. New York: William Morrow and Co., 1979.

Sher, Barbara and Gottlieb, Annie. *Wishcraft: How to Get What You Really Want*. New York: Viking Press, 1979.

Weaver, Peter A. *You, Inc.: A Detailed Escape Route to Being Your Own Boss*. New york: Doubleday & Co., 1975.

Winston, Sandra. *The Entrepreneurial Woman*. New York: Newsweek Books, 1979.

BOOKLETS

Profiles of Urban Business, 30¢ each, can be obtained from the Superintendent of Documents, U.S. Government Printing Office, Washington, D.C. 20402.

Small Business Reporter, published by the Bank of America, consists of
54 business profiles, $1 each. You can obtain the list from the Bank
of America, Department 3210, Box 37000, San Francisco, CA 94137
or from Bank of America, Department of Communications and
Public Affairs, 37–41 Broad Street, New York, NY 10004.

A number of small business booklets—"Starting a Business after Fifty" "How to Make Money Selling at Flea Markets and Antique Fairs,"
and "How to Turn Your Ideas into Dollars," and many more—are
published by Pilot Books, 347 Fifth Avenue, New York, NY 20026.

OTHER RESOURCES

If personal recommendations are not fruitful you can get *lawyer's* names
from state bar associations or from the Martindale-Hubbell Legal Directory which describes lawyers' specialties, lists them by cities and
gives colleagues' evaluations.

For *women lawyers,* good sources are your local university law
schools, feminist organizations or *A Directory of Women Attorneys* with
the names of more than 5,000 practicing lawyers throughout the country.

The *Economic Development Administration* of the U.S. Commerce
Department (EDA). Twelve EDA research and development centers
throughout the country provide management and technical assistance
to small businesses and help in finding capital and developing loan
practices. They work through universities to provide assistance in setting up businesses. For a list of their pamphlets—or to locate the EDA
center nearest you—write to Economic Development Administration,
225 Broadway, New York, New York 10007, Attention Public Affairs.

State Commerce Departments and *City Chambers of Commerce* publish
booklets that can provide help on tax and insurance requirements in
your area. Watch for business seminars conducted under the auspices
of your local Chamber of Commerce.

Through their *continuing education programs,* many state and city
colleges and universities offer courses in starting a business as well as
courses in a variety of business management skills.

The Small Business Administration (SBA) offers management assistance publications available through regional offices. Their checklist for "Starting Your Own Business" and a number of other booklets are available free or at a nominal charge.

The SBA also runs management assistance conferences, workshops, clinics, and individual counseling programs conducted by management assistance officers in 96 field offices. Check the phone books under "U.S. Small Business Administration" or write directly to the Small Business Administration, 1441 L Street, N.W., Washington, D.C. 20416. A list of the 96 regional SBA offices is appended.

The *Association of Women Business Owners* (AWBO), which now has chapters in several cities, has developed a network of women in business who can provide advice to women starting similar businesses. The organization publishes a bimonthly bulletin. For further information, write to AWBO, 525 West End Avenue, New York, New York 10024.

The *First Women's Bank* (New York) runs seminars covering aspects of business ownership. For information write to First Women's Bank, 111 East 57th Street, New York, New York 10022.

There's more, much more. It's up to you to go out and find your own sources and resources. One doesn't need a crystal ball to know that the '80s will be a decisive decade for women as entrepreneurs. More of them will go into business—and more will succeed in the businesses they start. We hope you, the reader, will be one of them. Good luck!

INDEX

167

J

Jankowski, Evelyne, 37–39
"Jotul Stoves," factors of
    success, 24–25

K

Kulicke, Barbara, 31–32
Kulicke Design Group,
    factors of success,
    31–32
Kulicke, Robert, 31–32

L

"La Boutique," financing
    proposal, example,
    87–101
Lawsuits, 62–63
Leases, 61–62. *See also*
    Proposal for
    financing, example
    health codes, awareness
    of, 108
    negotiation of,
    guidelines for, 109
Legal procedures. *See*
    Attorneys
Legal requirements,
    employee hiring, 119
Liability insurance, 69. *See
    also* Leases; Proposal
    for financing, example
Licenses, business, 27, 62

Loans. *See also* Funding,
    sources of; Financial
    record keeping
    interest rates, 84
    long term, 81
    short term, 82
Location of business
    accessibility, 110–111
    competition, awareness
        of, 82
    cost, 106–107
    home office, 103–104
    selection, 104–109
    targeting customers,
        105–106
Los Angeles Women in
    Business, 138

M

Mailing sevice, 103–104
Mailing, use of in
    advertising, 25–27,
    33, 38, 140–141
Marketing Strategies. *See
    also* Advertising;
    Needs, perception of;
    Needs, targeting of;
    Public Relations;
    customer climate,
        52–53
    economic influence on,
        52–53
    environmental influence
        on, 24–25, 27–29, 52